You Are Not Alone

You Are Not Alone

Encouragement for the Heart of a Military Spouse

30 Days of Readings

Jen McDonald

You Are Not Alone

ISBN 978-0-9836477-2-0
Published by Injoy, Inc. **www.injoyinc.com**

Cover design by Laurel Popejoy of Pure Image Photography and Graphics, www.pureimagegraphics.com

Dedication

"Trust in the Lord with all your heart, and lean not on your own understanding; in all your ways submit to him, and he will make your paths straight" (Proverbs 3:5,6).

The above is what I would consider my "life verse" and I am thankful that, though I can't always see the path in front of me, God does, and he has been faithful to his promise to lead me through all the twists, turns, and challenges life has thrown at me.

To my husband, Steve. I don't even know where to begin. Thank you for your love and friendship through all these years, for putting up with my impatience and emotions that you didn't necessarily understand, for all the times you ran to the store even when you didn't feel like it, for putting gas in my car, for making me feel pretty when I was overdue with your baby, for not caring when I served you frozen pizza again because I was busy writing, for the late nights, for all the mandated military separations (yes, even those) so I'd remember how much I love and need you, for all the inside jokes and movie quotes, and for embracing me fully for who I am and never trying to change me (much). I love you so much. I can't imagine life without you, and guess what? You're my best buddy.

For my children Matthew, Gabriel, Grace, and Anna, and to my daughters-in-law Jeramae and Brittney, who are also military brats...you didn't get to choose this life and while I don't gloss over the challenges you've faced, you all are the true picture of hope, flexibility, and strength. I love who you are and the adults you've become. I admire you so much. Even if we weren't related, I'd want to know you. I love you.

Contents

Dedication iii

About Jen McDonald vii

What Others Are Saying About *You Are Not Alone* viii

Intro xiii

My Identity As a Military Spouse 1

Day 1: Lost but Not Alone 3

Day 2: Who Am I? 7

Day 3: The Dependent: What About Me? 13

Day 4: Learning to Let Go 17

Day 5: Unfair Comparisons 23

Day 6: Giving Up Control 27

Day 7: But I'm a Strong, Powerful Woman 33

Day 8: It Never Fails 39

Day 9: When Your World Is Shaken 43

Military Spouse Friendships 49

Day 10: Homesick 51

Day 11: Unexpected Friends 57

Day 12: I Don't Make Friends 61

Day 13: Encourage Each Other 65

Military Marriage 71

Day 14: Feed the Fish 73

Day 15: Called to Serve 77

Day 16: The Military Didn't Issue a Spouse 83

A Life of Transition: Moving with the Military 89

Day 17: Living in the Pause   91

Day 18: Lessons from Living Out of a Suitcase   95

Day 19: Embracing Where You Live   99

Separations: Dealing with TDYs and Deployments   105

Day 20: Goodbye, Again   107

Day 21: The Purple Wig   111

Day 22: When My Heart Is Overwhelmed   115

Day 23: Hello, Again   119

Day 24: Together Yet Apart   125

Military Families and Kids   131

Day 25: Lessons from My Military Kids   133

Day 26: Solo Parenting   139

Day 27: Maintaining Connections   145

God Is There in the Small Moments   149

Day 28: Searching for Beauty   151

Day 29: Roses in the Desert   155

Day 30: A Tapestry of Grace   161

Recommended Military Life Publications   167

Books Referenced   168

Endnotes   168

About Jen McDonald

Jen McDonald has been "married to the military" for 29 years, and is the mother of four, including one son in the military. She and her Air Force husband have been stationed all around the world from Europe to the Pacific and won't count how many houses they've lived in, because that would be too depressing.

She writes regularly for *Military Spouse Magazine*, and has been published in numerous books and national publications including *Good Housekeeping*, *Redbook*, and *Family Magazine*, as well as online sites such as Crosswalk.com and Focus on the Family's Family Talk Radio.

An experienced editor, she currently serves as the Content Editor for MilitaryByOwner Advertising. Her passion is to connect with and encourage other military spouses, whether it's through her writing or in real life. She also regularly writes about military life, parenting, and homeschooling.

Connect with Jen at her site, **jenmcdonald.net**, as well as on Facebook (jenmcdonaldwriter) and Twitter and Instagram @jenmcdonald88

What Others Are Saying About
You Are Not Alone

"Jen McDonald is a top-notch writer and military spouse, whose words often bring tears and laughter of reliability all within the same sentence. For years, she has been delighting audiences with the knowledge that they are not alone on this journey. Once again, she does it here."

Kate Dolack, Editor-in-Chief, *Military Spouse Magazine*

"*You Are Not Alone: Encouragement for the Heart of a Military Spouse* is the kind of devotional that speaks authentically to the heart, because Jen McDonald writes transparently from her experiences as a military spouse. It gave me a much deeper appreciation for the relationship challenges facing those serving in the military—and those married to them. There is help in this book for the aches of life, wherever you serve."

Diana Waring, Air Force brat and Navy mom, author of *Beyond Survival, History Revealed, and Experience History through Music*

"It is not often that a book can reach the new military spouse as well as ones like myself whose spouses are nearing retirement, but *You Are Not Alone* has done just that. The author does a fantastic job of drawing you in with very transparent examples of her journey, has you ask yourself how you can grow or change, and closes with relevant Scripture and a thoughtful prayer.

This would have been great as a brand new Army wife, and yet here is EXACTLY what I needed as the looming retirement has me feeling unstable. *You Are Not Alone: Encouragement for the Heart of a Military Spouse* is exactly that--

an amazing encouragement grounded in experience, wisdom, and Scripture. I will be buying this for friends in all seasons of life."

Tara Howes, Army spouse and co-host of Military Life Radio

"How I wish I'd had this wonderful book to read when I was a young Army wife! Jen's words of wisdom would have been just what I needed to endure the long days of TDY and solo parenting! Drawing on her experiences from living around the world, her stories are engaging and her down-to-earth encouragement is like having coffee with a dear friend. I especially love the challenging thoughts at the end of each story. This is one of those books I will return to again and again for inspiration."

Karen Campbell, author of *The Joy of Relationship Homeschooling*, thatmom.com

"I just got a peek into Jen McDonald's book, *You Are Not Alone: Encouragement for the Heart of a Military Spouse*. What a sweet breath of life! As a military spouse facing our 30-year retirement soon, I wish I had found this book years ago. Reading it was like sitting down for coffee with a dear friend and finding encouragement for the issues of this crazy military life. When she writes of the lessons she learned in the loneliness of being lost in a new location and the difficulties of single parenting through a deployment, my heart ached at the memories this surfaced for me. Jen's words laced with wisdom, grace, and humor are the balm my soul needed.

This is a book written of her military spouse experience because that is the life she is living, but the truths found in here transcend all walks of life. These are nuggets of truth mined from a life well lived. I'll be giving this as a gift to many young spouses who are beginning this amazing journey!"

Terri Laurent, Air Force spouse

"I found the daily readings so relatable. Jen McDonald was able to take these little situations and experiences in life and make them teachable moments! The "Basic Training for Spouses" area is wonderful. I found the simple exercises and challenges easy to apply to everyday life to better yourself and your marriage. The encouragement of these daily readings is priceless.

As a "seasoned" (maybe over seasoned) spouse, it was easy to forget the little things you can do to stay encouraged. Being able to gain encouragement and strength from your experiences is a gift! Thank you for sharing your years of knowledge and experience."

Penny Everett, Navy spouse (retired)

"Reading *You Are Not Alone: Encouragement for the Heart of a Military Spouse* touched me in a way few books do. As I read page after page, I kept thinking, "Oh my goodness, she is living my life!" or "Yes! That is EXACTLY how I felt!" There is a kinship that military spouses have, and reading this book of encouragement brought that home for me. What sets this book apart from others is the integration of personal stories, stories a vast majority of spouses can relate to, along with the "basic training," the scripture, the "think about it" sections and ending in prayer. No other book for military spouses comes close to touching my heart like this one did. This is a book you will want to keep next to your heart for many years to come."

Cindy Burlingame, Marine Corps spouse

"These modern parables not only resonate with the rookie spouse but also veteran spouses. It's so refreshing to know that everyday struggles, no matter how small, are not a singular battle but rather experienced on varying levels throughout the military community. This book serves as a collective voice to military families, even those who confront silent struggles-I absolutely loved it and found long overdue comfort in each paragraph."

Morgan Slade, Army spouse, freelance writer/photographer at Morgan Slade Photography

"Jen has shared straight from the heart good advice a good friend would give! Her honesty and transparency are so valuable in a culture where protocol, rank, and status can build walls."

Mardi Savage, Producer, New Hope Oahu TV; *Under the Blood Red Sun* Associate Producer

"Genuinely inspiring, *You Are Not Alone: Encouragement for the Heart of a Military Spouse* provides just that--encouragement for those living the unique nitty-gritties of military family life.

As the spouse of a retired military man and a mother of six, I highly recommend this book! I could so relate to the author's brief personal stories, it was as if she had been peeking into my own life stories and experiences. Each daily reading is short, personal, and practical, and her "Basic Training for Spouses" and "Think About It" sections inspire any of us to be proactive in our responses to the unique challenges we face as military spouses. Hope-filled, this book will inspire courage and faith in military spouses who daily live with a greater understanding of the word "sacrifice."

Mary Lyons, Air Force spouse

Intro

Welcome, dear military spouse. You don't realize it yet, but you're my hero. I hope you'll realize that by the time you finish this book. I'm so thankful you're here.

When I started this project, it was intended to be a memoir of sorts. I quickly realized that, though sharing stories can be fun, talking about the hard times, shared experiences, and even the joys of military life make more sense to me with a practical takeaway. I hope this can be that for you.

While I certainly hope you're able to relate to the stories I share, I included these sections in each daily reading in hopes of being a help: Basic Training for Spouses, related Scripture, Think About It (journal prompts), and a short guided prayer. You see, the other realization I had was that leaving out my faith when I look back over the past decades would not be authentic to who I am or to what has happened in my life. Each section is yours to use or not use as you see fit. If you're not a person of faith, I still hope that this book will speak to you on some level.

One note about journaling. I've included a limited amount of space after the "Think About It" questions, if you're prompted to jot some brief notes while you're reading. There are also some blank pages at the end of most of the sections for you to use for additional journaling space. If you need more space, my hope is that you will use the prompts for more detailed journaling in a personal journal to write out your thoughts, hopes, dreams, and goals.

I would love to connect with you, and especially hear if this book has been a help to you. If there's something I could do better, please let me know that, too! Find me at jenmcdonald.net

Finally, please know that you don't walk this path alone. The bond between military spouses is like no other, and we're here for you.

God bless you,

Jen McDonald

My Identity As a Military Spouse

Day 1: Lost but Not Alone

"There are far, far better things ahead than anything we leave behind." -C.S. Lewis

I'm going to murder him, I thought darkly as I rounded yet another unfamiliar corner in my little Subaru. A new arrival to the area and hopelessly lost, I found myself driving in circles through an inner city neighborhood. It seemed endless to this small-town girl, and honestly, a bit scary.

Earlier in the day, I'd shown my husband the route I intended to take to my job interview for a staff nurse position at a large teaching hospital downtown—the route the charge nurse had laid out for me on the phone.

"Why don't you go this way instead?" Steve said, showing me what looked to be a straight road nearly to the door of the hospital. (I've since learned to be a little bit wary when I hear those words from him now, but I hadn't learned this lesson yet!)

"Well...she said to go *this* way." I traced the map with my finger.

"But look! This goes right across and cuts off at least ten minutes," said my ever-optimistic husband. "You'll get there so much faster!"

It seemed logical and straightforward at the time, yet here I was. *Lost.* The road we'd studied on the map had not yet finished construction in real life, so the exit I needed was nonexistent. As this was in the days before GPS or cell phones, I had no clue where to go. I'd driven around so much that I couldn't even retrace my route back home, and the only payphone I'd passed was surrounded by a seedy-looking group of men, so onward I drove. It was now twenty minutes past the time I should have arrived at the hospital. I pulled over by a weedy, crumbling sidewalk, laid my head on the steering wheel, and cried frustrated tears.

What was I doing here? I didn't belong. I longed for the bright sunshine, rugged mountains, and blue skies of my native New Mexico. Here in Ohio, in the cold grey mid-winter, I felt suffocated by the closely-grouped buildings as much as by my loneliness. Driving aimlessly through an unfamiliar neighborhood seemed symbolic of everything in my life at the moment.

Lifting my head, I rummaged in my purse for a tissue. As I wiped my eyes, I noticed an overpass a few blocks down. Could it be? The highway I needed? It was. Miraculously picking the right onramp (I truly have a hopeless sense of direction), I made it to my interview thirty minutes past the appointed time. Hoping the charge nurse wouldn't notice my reddened eyes, I was surprised to be hired on the spot. I will chalk that up to the nursing shortage at the time and the hospital's desperation for staff—even interviewees arriving half an hour late! And yet…the empty spot in my heart would remain for some time.

As I look back on that young girl through the hindsight of nearly three decades as a military wife, I'm struck by the fact that *I didn't know what I didn't know.* I didn't even know enough to realize what questions I ought to be asking! Yet, like that young nurse who stumbled across the right exit onto the highway, I've often stumbled across answers and help just when I needed it. God is good like that. Through the years, I've been blessed by wonderful friends, military spouses who've freely offered their friendship and mentored me. I've witnessed some bad examples of what not to do, and I've even figured out a few things on my own.

I trust that, if you picked up this book, your own heart may be in some need of encouragement and help. Thank you for joining me! Let's walk this path together. If you're feeling lost and overwhelmed by the unwanted transitions you face as a military spouse, hang in there.

My hope is to encourage your heart and whisper to you, "You've got this!"

Because you do. You're just awesome.

Scripture

Not that I speak in regard to need, for I have learned **in whatever state I am,** to be content" (Philippians 4:11, NKJV, emphasis mine).

How handy of the Apostle Paul to write that just for me! In all seriousness, whether it's a state (or country!) or state of being, it's an important lesson.

"Forget the former things; do not dwell on the past. See, I am doing a new thing! Now it springs up; do you not perceive it?" (Isaiah 43:18).

Think About It

What is currently your biggest challenge in your life as a military spouse?

Pick a quote or Scripture that encourages you and write it at the end of this reading. When you begin to feel discouraged, read it!

Do you remember your first feelings as a military spouse? Were you completely lost like I was, confident, or something else?

Prayer

Dear Lord,

You have brought me to this place in life as a military spouse. Help me to embrace your will for my life and learn to trust that you will walk with me each step of the way, and that, no matter how lonely I feel in the moment, I am never alone because you are with me.

Amen

Day 2: Who Am I?

"The journey of reinvention is one of raw emotions

Emerging from dormancy

Surprising as a paper cut

Overwhelming as a hailstorm."

-Dave Rudbarg

She sidles quietly into the back of the meeting room, eyes flitting from one face to another in hopes of a mutual flash of recognition, of some spark of connection, but there is none. She is alone and knows no one at the spouses' meeting and wonders if she can muster up the courage to make friends again...

Another stands beside her car, attempting to console her sobbing preschooler who has just said goodbye to his father for yet another deployment...

That one walks into a job interview, bracing herself for the inevitable questions about why she's held five jobs in as many years. How can she convince the prospective employer that she is reliable and not a job-hopper?

The young mom is weary of others thinking they understand military life because they've watched Army Wives. *She also wants them to realize that while important, military life is not all that defines her. She longs to know and be known as simply **herself.***

So...who exactly *is* this military spouse? It's extremely difficult to put your finger on just what constitutes a "typical" military spouse, because simply put, there is no such thing. Like I once was, many spouses are scared young college students without a real perspective on what military life truly involves. Others are veterans or currently on active duty themselves. Some are older, perhaps on their second marriage, and already have children who are wholly unfamiliar with the demands and challenges of military life. And guess what else? She's not always a *she*. Since this is not my experience, I won't presume to understand your particular challenges by speaking to this directly, though I hope that my perspective can be useful for any spouse.

Military service affects the entire family, and will most likely impact each member in both positive and negative ways, some more strongly than others. Most of us are struggling with that balance of living out our own dreams and passions while being supportive spouses. And I'm not gonna sugarcoat it; it's downright *not fun* at times. Sometimes I am mad at the military, at Uncle Sam, even at regular citizens who don't have a clue of the demands placed on our family. Anyone in a family with a long-serving military member can't help but be changed by the effects of that service.

My oldest son is now serving in the Air Force. This makes me the mother-in-law of a military spouse! She was raised as a military "brat," and while she understands many of the nuances of military life, she still finds herself with questions, because being a military *spouse* is a different proposition altogether: *How will this affect my life? How will I have a career? Will I make friends? How will I continue to be...me? Will anyone ever look at me again and just see me for myself?* We're going to work through it together. You, me, and my daughter-in-law!

Basic Training for Spouses

The only thing I can truly be sure about is my identity in Christ. That is who I am; that is what I cling to. Everything else in my life could be gone in a second. In the wise words of Carol Barnier:

"If you've never had your life shaken, count your blessings. But for most of us in this world, bad things happen. Jobs are lost. Children are hurt. Spouses die. Spouses leave. Car accidents happen. Families grow apart. People dear to us become estranged...

So after I took all these things away, I looked in my heart, I looked at my core, and way off in the back, sitting in the shadows, waiting quietly with a patient smile on His face, sat Jesus, the Author and Perfecter of my faith. He met me right where I was...not where I should have been." [1]

Scripture

"Before I formed you in the womb I knew you, before you were born I set you apart" (Jeremiah 1:5).

"How great is the love the Father has lavished on us, that we should be called children of God! And that is what we are! The reason the world does not know us is that it did not know him. Dear friends, now we are children of God, and what we will be has not yet been made known. But we know that when he appears, we shall be like him, for we shall see him as he is" (1 John 3:1-2, NLT).

"Now you are the body of Christ, and each one of you is a part of it" (1 Corinthians 12:27).

Think About It

What one word springs to your mind first when you think about your identity? Is it a job or another role? Is there a part of that you need to surrender to the Lord?

Is there anything you need to overcome in order to make your own peace with the military?

What's the most surprising thing you've found out about yourself as a military spouse, whether your journey has been long or only just beginning?

Prayer

Dear Lord,

Thank you for accepting me as I am right now, not where I think I should be. Help me to stake my identity in you, regardless of circumstances. Thank you for giving me the strength to face each new day.

Amen

Day 3: The Dependent: What About Me?

> "Don't walk behind me; I may not lead. Don't walk in front of me; I may not follow. Just walk beside me and be my friend." -Albert Camus

Have you heard the old cringe-worthy saying, "If the military wanted you to have a spouse, they would have issued you one"?

I remember the first time I was called a *dependent*. Yikes. With no military background to draw from, I felt marginalized as though someone had patted me on the head like a small child. While the term *dependent* simply means someone who's entitled to the benefits, privileges, and rights that come with being married to or one who is the child of a service member, we can feel anything *but* dependent as we deal with forging a life not on our terms.

While I get why many of us feel the term *dependent* is demeaning and belittling, how about turning this term on its head a little bit? I *am* dependent on my spouse. And he is dependent on me. *That's kind of what marriage is designed for, isn't it?* If I ever get to a place where I feel no need for my husband, I think that would be a scary place. Everyone in our family relies on the others. We each bring our strengths and weaknesses to the family, and are truly *dependent* on each other.

Basic Training for Spouses

Many of us find we need to make career changes due to military life or give up our careers completely. My own career path has morphed through the years: I began as a Registered Nurse, stayed home raising children and homeschooling for many years, and now homeschool my youngest while working in a "virtual office" at home as a writer and editor. Here are a few tips I've gathered along the way:

At-home parents: It seems to me that there's a higher percentage of stay-at-home parents in the military community than in the civilian population. Many military families choose to have one parent at home to provide stability and care for the children, some stay home for a season waiting for licensure to transfer, while others find themselves unable to find work in their chosen field due to being at a remote or overseas location. This can actually end up being a blessing in disguise. When the military member has a constantly changing schedule or travels a lot, it makes sense for one parent to be more available. Yet, without a job to go to every day, it may be difficult to connect with other adults! What to do if you're the lone parent staying at home on your whole block?

- Go where the kids are: the playground, the pool, the park. That's where you'll meet other parents!
- Walk back and forth with your kids to school.
- Stay and watch dance class or soccer practice rather than dropping off.
- Hit the story hour at the nearest library or sign your children up for swimming lessons.

- You can even meet potential friends (they just don't know it yet!) at Starbucks!
- If that fails, start knocking on doors and introducing yourself to your neighbors. (Bringing goodies helps, too!)

Working parents: It can be singularly frustrating to leave a great job and start all over at a new location due to a military assignment. Many spouses struggle to find a new position or are forced to start over again at the bottom of the ladder of a new company when they'd been successful at their previous job. Others face childcare issues while juggling schedules with a spouse who's deployed or working night shifts.

One of the top concerns military spouses cite is difficulty keeping a career afloat. Do you know about career resources for military spouses? See the resources appendix for more!

Networking: One of the best kept secrets is how much networking can go on with other spouses. So-and-so heard of a job and tells you about it and it's the perfect fit.

Volunteer: If you're volunteering in any capacity, keep track of those hours and responsibilities. This will all translate well to a résumé.

Whatever path you choose, **don't give up.** Support is out there and you don't have to go this alone!

Scripture

"Walk with the wise and become wise, for a companion of fools suffers harm" (Proverbs 13:20).

"A friend loves at all times, and a brother is born for adversity" (Proverbs 17:17, NKJV).

"As iron sharpens iron, so one person sharpens another" (Proverbs 27:17).

Think About It

What do you feel when you hear the word *dependent* applied to you? Anger, defensiveness, or something else? How can you turn those feelings into something positive?

Are you looking for a job or career change, or do you desire to be at an at-home parent? List some concrete steps you can take to further your goals right now (taking classes, pursuing certification, visiting the career counselors on your installation, résumé writing, putting aside a set amount into savings each month, etc.).

Prayer

Dear Lord,

I pray that you will show me your will as I take each step in life, whether it's in an outside job or caring for my family. Help me lift up others and be a source of encouragement and not discouragement. And above all else, I ask that you remind me of my dependence on you each day.

Amen

Day 4: Learning to Let Go

"It has long been an axiom of mine that the little things are infinitely the most important." -Sir Arthur Conan Doyle

I don't like change.

This probably has to do with the fact that I spent my growing-up years in the same town, surrounded by grandparents, aunts, uncles, and cousins. I *liked* that life; it was all I knew.

So, it's a bit ironic to find myself now a military spouse of several decades. I've learned quickly that I am not in charge of anything as the military dictates my husband's schedule, where we'll live (the last few assignments have required us living on base), and even little things like what day I'll cut my grass!

My grandmother had a saying when things weren't going so well that had been passed on by her mother:

"If you can't change the world, you can move the furniture."

When she'd come up with that phrase, I'd scratch my head, wondering what in the world she could mean. Of course, now I get it. The idea is that when you can't control what's going on around you, make a change in your little corner of the world and you'll feel better!

Rearrange the furniture...go for a walk...cut your hair...try a new recipe...read a new book...start a new hobby.

Learning to let go of what I think *should be* has been one of my most difficult lessons as a military spouse. I have little control over what happens in my life. But if you stop and think about it, none of us really has any; it's only an illusion. Perhaps military spouses are forced to accept this truth in a concrete way on a more regular basis than some, but sooner or later each person faces this harsh reality through the normal course of life: illness, death, the effects of others' choices.

My great-grandmother, Gladys, the originator of the "move the furniture" phrase, was forced to accept many circumstances beyond her control. She lived through two world wars, her husband serving in WWI. She was a missionary to China as a young wife in the 1920s and delivered several of her children there, including her first, my grandmother. She walked down a mountainside at midnight to reach a midwife to deliver her baby. That's some woman!

Gladys also lost a son in his early adult years. That's a heartache I can only imagine. She saw her husband pass away before her and I'm sure had many other struggles I know nothing about. Yet she was remembered by her children as a loving mother, friend, writer, and gardener extraordinaire. She obviously took the time in the midst of her busy and challenging life to cultivate beauty, love, and friendship.

What does this mean for me, in the midst of my current unchosen situation? We've recently PCS'ed again, left behind great friends and a church family, and feel deeply the thousands of miles separating us and our two grown children.

What does it mean for you in whatever you're facing today? You may be thinking, like I do sometimes,

I don't like it, I didn't choose this, it's not fair…

Basic Training for Spouses

Acceptance. I read something simple yet profound recently. The gist of it was, we can deal with anything once we accept it. I cannot control what happens to me, but I *can* deal with my reaction to it.

It's ok to be sad. Sometimes you have to look back a bit in order to move forward. There are friends and places you will always miss and that's ok. Grieve those losses. After a move is an especially difficult time. When I'm having a down day, I'll tell my husband, "I'm going to feel what I feel today!" This gives me permission to be sad. It also puts a limit on it as well--this won't last forever.

Find something to be thankful for today. Whether or not you love your present circumstances, take a moment to find *one* thing today to be thankful for. **One** thing--you can do this!!

Scripture

"That's why *I take pleasure in my weaknesses,* and in the insults, hardships, persecutions, and troubles that I suffer for Christ. For when I am weak, then I am strong" (2 Corinthians 12:10).

"I can do everything through him who gives me strength" (Philippians 4:13).

"He gives strength to the weary and increases the power of the weak. Even youths grow tired and weary, and young men stumble and fall; but those who hope in the LORD will renew their strength. They will soar on wings like eagles; they will run and not grow weary, they will walk and not be faint" (Isaiah 40:29-31).

Think About It

Trusting in God's promises might seem like a "small thing," like moving the furniture. It is amazing what he can do with such little faith on our part! What little thing can you trust God with today?

Is there one part of military life that you've decided you can't do?

List one simple thing that you can do to "move the furniture" in your present situation.

Prayer

Dear Lord,

I may not like where you've chosen to place me at this time. I don't always understand your ways or what you're asking of me. Help me to trust your heart and call to mind all the times you've been faithful to me in the past. I know that your plans toward me are loving and that even the challenging times are needed as you continue your work in me.

Amen

Day 5: Unfair Comparisons

"Don't compare your behind-the-scenes with everyone else's highlight reel." –Unknown

A particular child of mine was having a difficult time adjusting to our latest move and let me know it in no uncertain terms. Words like, "Why did I have to move? I wish I could have stayed behind with our friends!" were thrown at me on a regular basis.

Her feelings--and even words--mirrored my own. After arriving at our new base in the midst of a hot, sticky summer, my husband immediately began traveling with his new assignment, and the rest of us felt stuck in temporary billeting while we waited for housing. I was grieving the loss of our previous church family and dear friends, didn't like the part of the country we were in, and, frankly, had a bad attitude. If you'd asked me how I felt at that moment, I know I would have stated that the whole situation was unfair, not expected, and *unfair!*

There are moments when I feel downright discontent with the life I lead. Thoughts race: *Why do we have to keep moving? What would it be like for my children to be raised in the same town, knowing the same people their whole lives? Why are we stationed in this dumb place?*

Once I let myself go there, it's not long before I'm feeling entitled and crabby and it shows. I can tell I'm heading down a wrong path when all my prayers and thoughts feature *I-I-I* and *me-me-me*. I stop seeing the needs of others around me and become so self-focused that I'm sure I'm insufferable. (Surely I'm not the only one!)

One side note to these wandering thoughts is that some family members have admitted to feeling a little jealous of *our* lives. It struck me as so funny when I first heard this. While I was focused on the separations, the changeableness, and uncertainty that is ingrained into our lives, they were seeing the travel, the opportunities, the "worldliness" our kids have from living all over the globe. *Huh*. It's simply a matter of perspective, isn't it?

Basic Training for Spouses

When comparing military to civilian life, the "grass is always greener mentality" can take over. Your friends may have grandparents nearby, their spouse doesn't regularly travel, or they may seem to have more stability overall. Is there anything that can help when, like me, you find yourself slipping into the comparison mindset? While it may seem logical to tell yourself simply, *don't compare*, there are some days it's easier to do this than others.

What are some ways to consciously cultivate contentment?

Gratitude. Focusing on gratitude helped me make a drastic change in my attitude. It may feel artificial at first, but practice a daily exercise in finding just one thing to be grateful for and see what happens.

Realize everyone has some challenge. There is no point in comparing hardships with others. Everyone deals with something and it's been said that if you could see what burdens others carry, you'd go racing back to your own and realize they aren't so bad, after all.

Things are not always what they seem. It's tempting to look at other people's lives and feel convinced that we're coming up with the short end of the stick. This is a pointless exercise. There's no way for us to really know what others are going through behind closed doors.

Accept. Accepting what *is* keeps me from expending energy on things I can't change. Change what you can; accept the rest. There is freedom to be found in simply letting go of what we can't control.

Distract yourself. Honestly? Sometimes no amount of positive self-talk will help at a given moment. You simply have to work through the grief and challenges of change through the passage of time. Learn to distract yourself with new experiences.

For us, it meant getting out of billeting every day, even when we didn't feel like it, and exploring the surrounding area. It meant not letting my teen wallow under her covers too much, but encouraging her to get out. It meant not focusing on everything we'd lost and trying a new recipe or checking out the new library. None of these things solved the underlying issue, but in the words of Ma Ingalls from *Little House on the Prairie* who experienced lots of changes herself,

> "This earthly life is a battle. If it isn't one thing to contend with, it's another. It always has been so, and it always will be. The sooner you make up your mind to that, the better off you are, and the more thankful for your pleasures."

Focusing on something else for even a few minutes might take your mind off what you're contending with at the moment.

Scripture

"But godliness with contentment is great gain. For we brought nothing into the world, and we can take nothing out of it. But if we have food and clothing, we will be content with that" (1 Timothy 6:6-8).

"A joyful heart makes a cheerful face. But when the heart is sad, the spirit is broken" (Proverbs 15:13, NASB).

Think About It

Is there a particular area of life you find yourself comparing to others, which then causes you to feel discontent? What is it?

Choose one thing to be thankful for each day and write it here:

Prayer

Dear Lord,

I am trusting that you have brought me to where I am at this moment for a reason. Help me to trust your heart toward me even when it doesn't make sense on the surface. Teach me to look for things I can be grateful for today.

Amen

Day 6: Giving Up Control

"If you believe in a God who controls the big things, you have to believe in a God who controls the little things. It is we, of course, to whom things look little or big." -Elisabeth Elliot

"Mommy hammered the scorpion!" my five-year-old triumphantly announced as my husband walked in the door one evening from work. With raised eyebrows, my husband looked to me to explain this strange statement.

It hadn't been a pretty scene. That morning, our young children and I had made our way outdoors to enjoy some playtime before the hot Texas sun kicked in too strongly. As the toddler dragged his plastic trike across the garage floor, I saw it: the ugly, giant, *slimy* (ok, slimy might be a stretch) scorpion—my nemesis since moving into this house. I grabbed the nearest item to kill it, yes, a hammer, and violently ended the creature's existence. And with no remorse, I'll tell you.

Brand-new homeowners, we lived on the outskirts of town with plenty of space for our little ones to run and play. Something we hadn't realized, however, was that scorpions live in the ground in Texas (a fun fact I wish someone had mentioned!), and the construction of houses nearby was stirring them out of their own homes and into ours. A day rarely passed that I didn't find at least one scorpion: lingering by the front door, crawling up a wall, latched onto the outside of the house. *I had no idea that scorpions could scale walls.*

I hated them. I had nightmares about them. I smashed them viciously if I was home alone or shrieked like a small child if my husband was around. I worried that a scorpion would find its way into one of the children's beds and checked on the kids repeatedly during the night. We had exterminators come, but continued to find them. Battling nature in the middle of a desert is a lost cause!

One day, as my toddler trotted towards her play table, I noticed a dark shape inside one of the plastic sliding drawers. I snatched her chubby hands away before she could thrust them into the drawer within reach of—you guessed it—one of the biggest scorpions I'd ever seen. I cried in relief and frustration that day. It didn't seem like we could get away from them *any*where. Even my own living room wasn't safe.

The day I "hammered the scorpion" brought me a realization. The scorpions had become symbolic of everything I couldn't control, and they needed to be conquered.

There were so many things I couldn't control. Due to a recent move and Steve's work schedule while he finished classes toward his degree, I found myself often alone. We both stayed exhausted and most of my waking hours were spent with my young children. I loved being a stay-at-home mom, but the silence of the lonely evenings threatened to be my undoing.

I was not in control of anything.

I like being in control.

In the words of Jeff Manion, I'd found myself in "The Land Between," that "space where we feel lost or lonely or deeply hurt." Yet, I hadn't realized that it is also "fertile ground for our spiritual transformation and for God's grace to be revealed in magnificent ways."[2]

Basic Training for Spouses

I reached a point where I realized that my futile attempts at controlling my life--where we lived, our schedule, even how a given day would go--were just that...*futile*. Maybe you've reached that point in your own life. Perhaps it's something entirely different and you think battling a few scorpions would be a piece of cake in comparison to what you're dealing with.

There are no quick fixes when it comes to surrendering your life to God's will and being okay with his answers even if it's not what you'd prefer. I'm still walking through this and I imagine I will be as long as I live. There are a few things I try to practice and remind myself as I work on loosening my tight grasp over circumstances I cannot control. Maybe they'll help you, too.

Grab whatever moments you can find with God. As a Christian, I know the importance of seeking God each day. Yet, if I didn't find time for a devotion or quiet time in the early mornings, it felt like it didn't "count." Have you ever felt this way? I learned to snatch moments when I could—pondering a fragment of Scripture as I nursed the baby, praying for my children and husband as I folded their laundry, and turning on uplifting music as a background to our day.

Be honest. Do you know that God can handle your anger and questions? He already knows what you're feeling, so there is no sense in trying to hide it. The Bible is full of stories of people like David "crying out to the Lord." Many of us have been raised to think that we must only come to God respectfully and quietly. While I am not inviting disrespect, I do believe that honest feelings brought up in times of prayer are good and even necessary.

Not looking at every situation as a problem to be solved. There are circumstances that just *are*. God needed to show, and is still showing, this control freak the limits of what I can actually control. I am independent and feisty by nature, and am still learning the lesson that my fussing and nagging don't have the power to change anything. (Other than making everyone around me grumpy.)

Finding joy in the small things. When life is overwhelming, I remind myself of all that I have to be grateful for. Even if it's just one thing, can you find a bright spot in the midst of trying circumstances today?

Life didn't magically get better, but one day, I realized that I hadn't seen a scorpion in a while. As more and more houses went up, the pests were driven out into the desert instead of toward our house.

And, as time went on, I felt less of the old discontent and unhappiness rearing its ugly head within my spirit as I consciously built my own "house" of joy, thankfulness, and resting in God's will for my life.

I'd hammered the scorpion.

Scripture

"In my distress I called to the Lord; I cried to my God for help. From his temple he heard my voice; my cry came before him, into his ears" (Psalm 18:6).

"For we do not have a high priest who is unable to empathize with our weaknesses, but we have one who has been tempted in every way, just as we are—yet he did not sin. Let us then approach God's throne of grace with confidence, so that we may receive mercy and find grace to help us in our time of need" (Hebrews 4:15-16).

"As the deer pants for streams of water, so my soul pants for you, my God. My soul thirsts for God, for the living God. When can I go and meet with God?" (Psalm 42:1-2).

Think About It

What circumstance in your life is currently challenging you? Make it a matter of honest prayer and tell God how you really feel.

What "little thing" are you having a hard time trusting God with? What actions can you take this week to relinquish control over it?

Prayer

Dear Lord,

Remind me that you see the overall picture of my life from beginning to end. Give me perspective for my trying circumstances and help me find the good in every situation, even when it's hard to see. Remind me of your love for me and help me to turn to you in challenging times.

Amen

Day 7: But I'm a Strong, Powerful Woman

"A strong marriage rarely has two strong people at the same time. It is a husband and wife who take turns being strong for each other in the moments when the other feels weak."
-Ashley Willis

Many military wives are inspired by the image of Rosie the Riveter, the icon of women on the home front during the World War II era. I love that picture of strength and the "can-do" attitude of American women who picked up the slack for our country, working in factories and holding down responsibilities at home while our nation was at war. My grandmother was one of those left behind. Young and in love, my grandfather shipped off to Europe shortly after finding out they were pregnant with their first child, who happened to be my father. They had no idea how long they'd be apart, and when--or if--he'd return home.

She gave birth to that baby while he was overseas, and my grandfather didn't see his firstborn until the toddler was 18 months old. (And I think we've had long separations!) Grandma worked in a telegraph office, kept a "victory garden," and, like most of the country, scrimped and saved to help the troops overseas. When she'd later recall stories about this time, it was very matter of fact without a hint of self-pity. Just the facts. Yet, I can only imagine how difficult it must have been for her. She's my hero.

So with the picture of women like her or the larger-than-life Rosie in our minds, what happens when a spouse is truly struggling? There have been some tragic stories in recent times of young wives crumbling under the weight of deployment and separation who end up abusing or neglecting their own children. We've all known women who spent their husband's deployment partying or acting as if they were single again. Some can argue that we're spoiled Americans, that we're simply not used to being deprived of what we want, when we want it. While there may be some truth to that, what about the spouse who is trying her best, yet who can barely put one foot in front of another and is too ashamed to admit she is not doing well and could use some help?

Basic Training for Spouses

For those of who've been around the block a few times, I offer these suggestions.

Let's drop the "been there-done that" attitude: Sometimes we veteran spouses are too quick to swap our war stories or one-up each other. It can end up being like comparing labor and birth stories. "Oh, you had an eight-hour labor? Well, I had a 36-hour labor, which ended in a C-section!" It can be good fun to vent at times, but if we're so busy regaling others with what we've been through, a young spouse may be too fearful to admit she is struggling and doesn't know how she's going to do this *one more day*. It's good to remember this isn't a competition. The one with the worst story doesn't win.

Don't focus so much on being tough: Are we too quick to say (or have an attitude of) "Just put on your big girl panties and get over it?" By our words or actions, are we conveying that another's struggles aren't worth speaking about? I'm all for personal responsibility, for being strong and independent, for attempting to keep my sense of humor, for laughing at ridiculous circumstances (Murphy's law when hubby is gone), but I hope I have never made it impossible for someone to speak up who was truly floundering and in need of more than a laugh or "atta girl" speech.

Have we unwittingly created an atmosphere in which it's a failure to admit *we* need help? Are we so focused on being strong that we don't allow *ourselves* to admit when we could use a helping hand?

Seek help when you need it. It's no shame to admit you need a breather. Whether it's hiring a sitter for a few hours or snatching a nap when possible, it's important to build in time alone and be proactive vs. reactive. Some of us need to have time with friends; others must have quiet to recharge. There's no reward for not caring for yourself while your spouse is gone!

It's also helpful to know a chaplain or counselor familiar with military family struggles to turn to for help for yourself or others. (Free and confidential Military Family Life Counselors are available on most installations.) Sometimes, speaking with a counselor is enough to get through a rough patch. But other times, it's not enough and these professionals can make referrals for medical help. *It is no shame.*

Be a friend to others...but don't forget to also be kind to yourself.

Scripture

"Peace I leave with you; my peace I give you. I do not give to you as the world gives. Do not let your hearts be troubled and do not be afraid" (John 14:27).

"God is our refuge and strength, an ever-present help in trouble" (Psalms 46:1).

Think About It

During one of my husband's first deployments, Psalms 91 became my special Scripture. I read it daily and clung to its truths with all my heart. I hope you'll find your own to cling to during those moments when you need to shore up your faith. What are some Bible verses or quotes that encourage you?

Is there something you're struggling with today that you need help with? What steps will you take *today* to get practical help for your situation?

If you're doing fine, is there someone you know who could use a helping hand right now?

Prayer

Dear Lord,

Help me to recognize my need for you even when I feel I have to prove I can handle everything alone. Remind me to not only reach out to others, but to accept help when it's my turn. Thank you for your strength to face each new day.

Amen

Day 8: It Never Fails

"We cannot change our past... we cannot change the fact that people will act in a certain way. We cannot change the inevitable. The only thing we can do is play on the one string we have, and that is our attitude... I am convinced that life is 10% what happens to me and 90% how I react to it." -Chuck Swindoll

I still remember those famous last words I uttered to my husband on our arrival to North Dakota from our assignment in Guam: "Just get us through this first winter, *then* you can deploy." I figured that was reasonable. Since we'd been lucky enough to have two back-to-back sunny beach assignments, we hadn't been through a real winter in over five years. But wouldn't you know it? That first winter found him deployed and me wrestling with a snow blower and recalling how to maneuver my minivan down icy roads.

Military spouses quickly become experts at dealing with the unexpected. And just when we think we have a situation figured out, circumstances have a way of changing completely. I'm sure you can come up with your own examples. Whether it's a short-notice deployment, news that your spouse's unit is deactivating within months of arriving at a new assignment and you'll be moving on and not settling down like you thought; a school district giving you difficulties about your high schooler's credits from a previous school, starting over (again) at a new job--you fill in the blank!--it's often said that the only constant in this military spouse life is *change*.

A comfort in the midst of this constantly changing life is the knowledge that God's love never fails. When I'm overwhelmed, God cares. When I walk around a new city, unknown to every person I meet, he knows me. When I am crushed with grief over leaving behind dear friends, he meets me there in that sad place. And even when life is good and I don't feel my need of him as strongly, he waits patiently.

God's love never fails, regardless of my awareness of my need for him. And that is worth holding on to.

Basic Training for Spouses

There are times we can feel we've given up *too much* for this military gig: everyday moments and special occasions with extended family, the privilege of raising children in one place, even down to having the choice of where we live.

Beware of saying "I could do anything but *that*," because more often than not, that circumstance we attempted so hard to avoid becomes the very thing we end up facing! Flip things around and try to find a bright side to whatever unique-to-military-life challenge you're currently facing.

For instance, many spouses say they could live anywhere but _____. They couldn't possibly be expected to live in the frozen North because it's too cold or the South because it's too humid, overseas because it's too far from their extended family, or alone while a spouse deploys. Yes, it is challenging, but not impossible. Even in a locale you don't love, try to find at least *one* thing to be thankful for. Find something! Otherwise, your time in the dreaded location will be long indeed.

Scripture

"Give thanks to the Lord, for he is good. His love endures forever" (Psalms 136:1).

"Who shall separate us from the love of Christ? Shall trouble or hardship or persecution or famine or nakedness or danger or sword?...For I am convinced that neither death nor life, neither angels nor demons, neither the present nor the future, nor any powers, neither height nor depth, nor anything else in all creation, will be able to separate us from the love of God that is in Christ Jesus our Lord" (Romans 8:35, 38).

"Therefore, my dear brothers and sisters, stand firm. Let nothing move you. Always give yourselves fully to the work of the Lord, because you know that your labor in the Lord is not in vain" (1 Corinthians 15:58).

Think About It

Remind yourself of a specific way that God has met you in a challenging moment.

What's been the most surprising event in your military spouse life so far? How did God meet you there?

Prayer

Dear Lord,

Thank you that you always give me what I need, even when I don't know I need it! Thank you for walking through the ups and downs of my life right alongside me. I'm grateful that I am never alone, because of you.

Amen

Day 9: When Your World Is Shaken

"No man is an island." -John Donne

A train rumbled under my bed. Why was a train...*under my bed?* Suddenly waking, I saw the emergency lights in our hall flicker on and watched my husband trying to stand up and fall...stand up and fall..over and over. His feet didn't seem to work. I could hear cabinets slamming open in the background and the tinkling of glassware as it crashed to the ground. As I attempted to get out of my bed, the violent motion of the house threw me into my dresser. The floor undulated like something in a carnival funhouse and nothing made any sense. Laying on the shaking floor, catching my breath, I turned my head to see my three-year-old crawling through my doorway, Marine-style flat on her belly, making an unsteady beeline to me. Suddenly the shaking stopped. Heart racing, I heard someone's ragged breathing and realized it was my own. By then, my daughter had reached me and curled up on my chest, hiding under her blankie.

"Mom...Dad...what was THAT?" piped a little voice from the next room.

It was an earthquake.

Nothing had prepared me for the feeling that came with a 7.2 magnitude earthquake that hit our home on the island of Guam that night. Though we'd heard about the earthquakes in that part of the world, none of us had ever experienced one and we've certainly never felt one that strong again. Surprisingly, our house didn't sustain any major damage, but for days we experienced aftershocks and I'd jumpily grab a wall or a person nearby out of instinct. Even months later when we felt a tremor, I'd hold onto anything solid. But when I think back to that day, what stands out to me is the picture of my little daughter, doing everything in her power to get to safety--*me*.

Where do I turn when the circumstances of life shake me and nothing makes sense?

I call my sister.

I call my mom.

I text a friend.

I vent about it to my husband or my kids.

While there's obviously nothing *wrong* with talking to the people in my life, the earthquake has become an object lesson for me: *Get to God as quickly as you can.*

I don't do this perfectly; in fact, I would venture a guess that I still wait too long before turning to God with my problems. But the picture of childlike faith is so apt and a visual reminder of my need for him.

Basic Training for Spouses

Is there something in your life that's being shaken? Whether it's a circumstance unique to military life or not, know that God will walk through it with you. There are no quick and easy answers to navigating problems, but there are some tools you can use to strengthen your spiritual life. Consider the following:

A local church fellowship. It's very easy to become disconnected if you feel transient, or think you will only be stationed in a place for a couple of years, or have tried several churches and simply don't feel like you belong. *Keep trying.* You'll find your place! Not only will you benefit from regular church attendance, you'll also have opportunities for friendships, local outreach, and a sense of community. You need them; they need you.

Healthy friendships. If you're a person of faith, you simply need some like-minded friendships in your life. Who is pointing you back to what you deeply believe or holding you accountable? Who is encouraging you and likewise, who are *you* encouraging?

Small moments. Especially if you're raising small children, it may prove difficult to have concentrated "devotional" times. That's ok. Embrace this season of your life and find moments with God when you can: turn on praise music while doing mundane tasks or driving, pray as you accomplish household chores, talk with your children about God's goodness as you go about everyday activities. It counts! Building in small moments with God will only strengthen your faith.

Scripture

"Consider it pure joy, my brothers and sisters, whenever you face trials of many kinds, because you know that the testing of your faith produces perseverance. Let perseverance finish its work so that you may be mature and complete, not lacking anything. If any of you lacks wisdom, you should ask God, who gives generously to all without finding fault, and it will be given to you. But when you ask, you must believe and not doubt, because the one who doubts is like a wave of the sea, blown and tossed by the wind" (James 1:2-6).

"Let us hold unswervingly to the hope we profess, for he who promised is faithful. And let us consider how we may spur one another on toward love and good deeds, not giving up meeting together, as some are in the habit of doing, but encouraging one another—and all the more as you see the Day approaching" (Hebrews 10:23-25).

Think About It

Are you struggling to find other people who share your faith? What can you do to change that? Some ideas: check in with your base or post chapel for services or meeting times, or ask a neighbor what church they attend.

When you think about what your first response is when problems hit and pieces of your world feel like they're crumbling, be honest. Where do you turn first?

If you don't like the answer, what can you do to change it?

Prayer

Dear Lord,

I know that circumstances in my life will fall apart at times. Help me to turn to you for help and strength and realize that I can't solve everything by myself. Remind me of my need for others and that I need them even if I feel I can go it alone. Give me eyes to notice others around me and what I can do for them. Help me develop healthy relationships as we work to build each other up in our faith.

Amen

Military Spouse Friendships

Day 10: Homesick

"Maybe you had to leave in order to really miss a place; maybe you had to travel to figure out how beloved your starting point was." -Jodi Picoult

"Who is that man sitting in the foyer?"

I shifted uncomfortably in my seat. Even though I was surrounded by many women in the meeting room of the large church we attended, I felt isolated as I heard several ladies whispering about the strange man who sat alone in the dark entryway. I knew it seemed odd, so finally, I mustered up my courage and informed them that it was my husband.

What I didn't tell them? This was part of our "deal" to help me move on. We'd been at our first military assignment for a handful of months and I wasn't handling it well. Desperately homesick for my family, our church, and our old friends, I longed for what had been, which made it impossible to move forward. Perhaps a part of me figured if I gave in to my misery, I could somehow go home and have things the way they used to be. Looking back now, I recognize that I was going through the classic stages of grief: shock, denial, anger, and so on. It would be an understatement to say I did not initially embrace military spouse life.

I also didn't tell them what my husband had said--the words that had brought me to their meeting that day.

"I'm buying you a plane ticket home...one-way, if that's what you want."

Those words from my husband shocked me. He'd recognized how unhappy I was, and wondered if the solution was for me to go back home...*and stay there.* The realization of my self-absorption was the shock I needed to move forward. I'd committed to being married and needed to embrace life with just the two of us.

Since I was too shy to go to any of the spouses' groups through our church or the military (which would be laughable to anyone who knows me now), my husband offered to go along with me and wait outside if I would just try something. *Anything.* (I'm telling you, he was desperate!) So, he drove me to a women's Bible study and waited for me in the foyer through the two-hour meeting, while I made an awkward attempt at branching out.

How adorable is that!

Though times have changed and it's so much easier to become educated about military culture online, find a spouses' group through social media, and make connections, I believe there is something that hasn't changed—the lost feeling of being absorbed into this monolithic *thing* that is the world of the military, of wondering if you'll ever find your place in it. There will always be a part of us that longs for real-life friendship.

If I could go back and give that young woman some advice, I would tell her that *home* will take on a new meaning. *Home* will have more to do with the people you love and the life you create, rather than a specific location. Your feeling of *home* will probably be in several places at once. And homesickness will fade as you create a new sense of home, no matter where you happen to live. And I would tell her,

Hang in there. I promise this will get better.

Basic Training for Spouses

Exercise the art of positive thinking. Some of us have the "glass half full" mindset. While we like to think we're looking at life realistically, continuing to embrace detrimental honesty has the potential of turning into an unhealthy pattern. Proverbs 27:3 says, "As a man thinks in his heart, so is he…" I often have to force myself into thinking positively and taking action. Some areas that I needed to tackle were not complaining so much or immediately focusing on perceived negatives.

Reach out…strike up a conversation. You might create a new friendship--one not based on how long you've known someone.

Record your memories. It's important to remember where we've been and record our unique family history. Create digital scrapbooks or find some other way to memorialize your memories and places you've visited. I know one woman who creates a photo canvas from her family's favorite travels and has walls covered with memories! For you, maybe it's something as simple as a wall hanging with a list of the locations you've been stationed.

Take baby steps. It can seem like things will never get better. While in the course of writing this book, I began a running program (I have no idea why!). I couldn't get through a mile without walking when I first began. Now, after many months of continuing to put one foot in front of the other, I've successfully completed a 10k and find myself training for a half-marathon, something I could have never envisioned when I started! Realize that you don't have to know exactly how things will turn out--take baby steps now and trust that the path ahead of you will unfold as you persevere.

Time and patience heal a lot. Clichés are clichés because they have some truth to them. While it may not be helpful to you to hear right now that "time heals all wounds," please trust that it does. As does patience.

Scripture

"Turn to me and be gracious to me, for I am lonely…" (Psalms 25:16).

"Come to me, all you who are weary and burdened, and I will give you rest" (Matthew 11:28).

"God heals the brokenhearted and binds up their wounds" (Psalms 147:3).

Think About It

What part of *what was* do you find the hardest to let go?

Find one thing you like about your new location or circumstance and remind yourself of this. Repeat daily!

Prayer

Dear Lord,

Help me to remember that, even when I feel lonely, I am never truly alone because you are with me. Help me recognize the reminders of your presence each day. Remind me to lean on you when I feel abandoned and desolate.

Amen

Day 11: Unexpected Friends

"A friend is one that knows you as you are, understands where you have been, accepts what you have become, and still, gently allows you to grow." -William Shakespeare

I schlepped into the Tiny Tots ballet class late with two preschoolers in tutus and two not-happy-to-be-here boys in tow. I hurried my girls into the class, then perched on the bench facing the mirrored glass where we moms could observe our tiny ones making clumsy if not adorable attempts at twirling and pointing their toes. While settling down my boys with juice boxes and coloring books, a nearby lady struck up a conversation. She asked where my kids attended school and I mentioned that we homeschooled.

I'll never forget what happened next.

"You *homeschool*??" An inquisitive curly head popped out further down the row of quiet moms. At my affirmation, the woman practically elbowed her way to me! I wasn't sure if she was going to confront me about my educational choice or what, but what followed for the next hour (I'm sure to the annoyance of the other ladies on the bench) was a fast-paced, somewhat loud conversation, sprinkled with lots of laughter. Turns out she was a brand-new homeschool mom.

Tara and I have been friends ever since.

There are some people you just happen upon, recognize you are kindred spirits, and that is that.

I love those moments!

Basic Training for Spouses

Finding friends is not always so easy, but I've noticed over the years the types of friends that every military spouse needs at some point. Some people may be a combination of a couple of these traits. Hopefully, *you* will be one of these friends to someone, too.

The Go-Getter: She, like my friend Tara, does not hold back. You *will* be friends! She's the one who will plan play dates and organize field trips. She does not hesitate to call or text to check on you if she hasn't heard from you in a while. When you get short-notice orders, she'll be there with brownies and a checklist to help you organize. She seems to have boundless energy!

The Listening Ear: The one you'll turn to when you can't take one more day of a deployment or TDY, who is willing to drop everything to meet you for coffee so you can vent.

The Fun Friend: You *need* one of these! She'll go shopping, out to eat, or explore the area with you. She's willing to watch a sad movie and cry, just because you asked.

The Mentor: She's been around the block. She can help calm your fears when rumors abound about a deployed unit, provide much-needed perspective on military life, and reassure you that **your** kids won't be ruined because they're military brats.

The Civilian: This might surprise you, but non-military folk have ended up being some of my best friends. Especially if your spouse is in a high-ranking or highly visible job, it can be nice to get away from the "fishbowl" of military life and be with people who take you at face value. If you live off base, it can be a bit easier to make friends with civilians. For those living on a military installation, you'll have to make more of an effort—getting involved in a church or other community group to meet people. This friend will also help you remember the rest of the world doesn't revolve around the military! Often, these folks are key to introducing you to the local area and experiencing life 'outside the wire.'

Are you lonely? Look around. I'd bet there are some spouses who are just as lonesome as you are. There are potential friends all around. Sometimes it takes so little to reach out: take a chance, ask someone over for coffee, knock on a new neighbor's door, make a point of saying hello. Try it—you might be surprised!

Scripture

"A friend loves at all times, and a brother is born for adversity" (Proverbs 17:17).

"As soon as he had finished speaking to Saul, the soul of Jonathan was knit to the soul of David, and Jonathan loved him as his own soul. And Saul took him that day and would not let him return to his father's house. Then Jonathan made a covenant with David, because he loved him as his own soul" (1 Samuel 18:1-3 ESV).

Think About It

If you're having a difficult time making friends, what is holding you back from reaching out?

What can you do this week to make a new friend?

Are there friends you need to get back in touch with and let know how much they mean to you? What about nearby friends you need to reconnect with?

Prayer

Dear Lord,

Help me to cultivate the friendships you've planted in my life at this time. Don't let me be blind to opportunities to reach out to others who may need a friend. Thank you for all the friends you've placed in my life, both old and new.

Amen

Day 12: I Don't Make Friends

"It's friendship, friendship, just a perfect blendship

When other friendships have been forgit

Ours will still be it!"

-From the song "Friendship"

by Cole Porter

"I don't make friends," she said.

I was stunned. Was that even an option? As a young wife, I wasn't sure how to respond to this older woman that I was thrown together with frequently at military events. At that point, I'd been married to my Airman husband for a grand total of about 12 months.

She went on. *She'd done this thing for 20 years. She was tired of goodbyes. It was hard to know who to trust.* So her solution?

Don't make friends.

Though I was a shiny new military spouse, I knew enough to feel sorry for her. She was pleasant, but kept all of us at arm's length. I don't know what ended up happening to her. I hope she made peace and was able to get close to people again, somehow.

With the passing of (ahem) a lot of years, I understand better now. What I mean to say is that I can understand her feelings, but I've never been able to follow through and "just say no" to friends. An extroverted people person, I don't think I'm capable of it, actually. But yeah...I get it.

The hurt of saying goodbye doesn't get easier the more you do it; it seems to get more difficult. Probably because I know now how final it can be. I hate the goodbyes so much that I now refuse to say goodbye. "See you later" works better. Plus, with military life, you just never know.

But I've been blessed with so many different friends over the years. I've become fast friends with women I'd never have anticipated I'd hit it off with. Twenty years older than me or as many years younger...professional women, moms with master's degrees to those who barely finished high school, all manner of political leanings, different religions, and different backgrounds. *They're just beautiful.*

And I love them. They've added so much richness to my life. I wish I could gather them all up in one spot (they DO need to all meet each other!). What a hoot that would be! I hope you have your own circle of friends. If not–please keep trying!

Basic Training for Spouses

It's normal to be cautious with friendship, to feel the need to guard your heart a little bit. Perhaps the bigger question when making friends is not simply how to recognize and be open to new friends, but to learn how to *be* a good friend yourself. This will look different according to your personality, but there are a few common factors that form the basis of a great friendship, especially in the close-knit military community:

Recognize that you need others. "No man is an island." As much as military spouses pride themselves on being independent, you really aren't going to get far without the friendship of others. If nothing else, it makes the ride a whole lot more fun!

Be careful who you talk about. We all need a safe place to vent, but be careful about veering into gossip. Whoever listens to gossip *from* you will likely gossip *about* you.

Be able to set boundaries when necessary. Yes, we need each other, but keep your marriage as your first relationship priority.

Forgive quickly. Expecting the best and believing that people have the capacity to do better goes a long way towards smoothing out relationship issues.

Be willing to reach out and take a risk. In the military world, you'll find yourself meeting all sorts of different people from varying backgrounds. Someone who at first glance doesn't seem to be a person you'd have anything in common with may turn out to be your best friend ever. It's so worth it!

Scripture

"One who has unreliable friends soon comes to ruin, but there is a friend who sticks closer than a brother" (Proverbs 18:24).

"Dear friends, let us love one another, for love comes from God. Everyone who loves has been born of God and knows God" (1 John 4:7).

Think About It

When you consider the qualities of a friend, what is the most important to you?

What would you add to the list of what YOU want to be as a friend to others?

Prayer

Dear Lord,

I recognize that those who are in my life right now are those that you have placed there for a reason. Help me to not only seek out others for friendship for myself, but to learn to be a good friend to others. Let me see beyond the surface and be willing to get to know my friends more deeply.

Amen

Day 13: Encourage Each Other

"Kind words can be short and easy to speak, but their echoes are truly endless." -Mother Teresa

We'd been married a whole 18 months when my husband came home to tell me he'd been reassigned to another base and we'd be moving across the country in just a couple of months. Looking back at my reaction now, I have to laugh when I remember how I looked at him blankly and said with great sincerity,

"Can't you tell them it's not a good time right now?"

After all, we'd known families who'd been stationed in the same location five, eight, even ten years! I'd assumed it would be the same for us and wasn't ready to pick up and move just yet. To say I had no understanding of the inner workings of the military would be putting it mildly. After talking with several more seasoned military spouses, I discovered that a short-notice move like this was not a rarity and being ready to adapt to the latest changes of military life was a skill I'd need to cultivate. I'm so grateful for their kind understanding and help for that young spouse. If they'd laughed at me or otherwise shamed me, I doubt I would have ever reached out to a military spouse again. Instead, they realized how little I knew and helped me along gently.

Just recently, I woke up in the middle of the night in an empty bed. Again. Though we've now been married over 25 years, the loneliness at being apart, the frustration of frequent moves, the toll of military life on myself and my children still takes me by surprise at times. But, unfortunately, I've noticed a difference in the past few years. Where once a young (or old one, like me) spouse could reach out and look for support, lately there's been an increase in social media and even real life shaming of military spouses. You don't have to look too far to see it. And unfortunately, we've lost something along the way. Many spouses are reluctant to ask questions that I think we all deal with at some point: *Is what I'm feeling normal? Should I miss him this much? Why are my kids struggling?*

I've always thought of the military spouse community as a place of support and help. I hope you do, too. But if you're not finding that to be the case, is there anything you and I can do to change the climate?

Basic Training for Spouses

Kindness. I've been so touched by the kindness of others in my life. An unexpected call, a friend dropping by when I've felt alone, even a text or email has made more difference than the person sending them may have ever known. But kindness takes time. And some days seem to bring more tasks than time. If you're like me, getting caught up in the busyness of life is a temptation. But taking cookies to a new neighbor or noticing that I haven't seen a friend in a while and checking on her is important. It's no badge of honor to be so caught up in "busy" that I don't have the time for real-life relationships.

Sticking up for each other. I know several military spouse writers who've taken on the culture of military spouse bullying that seems to be prevalent on social media lately (if you don't know what I'm referring to, I'm glad!). Especially for inexperienced spouses, knowing that others have got their back can be a lifesaver. This can also apply in a group setting.

Paying it forward. Are you familiar with programs like HeartLink, an Air Force program for military spouses who've been married less than five years? I've so enjoyed sitting at a table and sharing with these young spouses. They benefit from having their questions about military acronyms answered. But I also benefit from their enthusiasm and energy! If others have invested in you, I hope you'll pass that along to those coming along behind as you grow into becoming a 'seasoned' spouse, whether it's through a formal program like HeartLink or a chat over a cup of coffee.

We need each other. When I'm having difficulties settling into a location, it can be tempting to depend on social media or long-distance friends for interaction. I'm so glad those outlets exist, as they've been a lifeline for me at certain points. However, there is nothing like real-life support. Hebrews 10:25 says, "Don't stop meeting with other believers" and there's a reason. Sometimes you just need that real-life conversation or even kick in the pants. I know I do! There's nothing quite like the honesty of a true friend.

Scripture

"One who has unreliable friends soon comes to ruin, but there is a friend who sticks closer than a brother" (Proverbs 18:24).

"A true friend is always loyal, and a brother is born to help in time of need" (Proverbs 17:17, TLB).

Think About It

Have you noticed a difference in the way military spouses relate to each other in recent years? If you feel it's for the worse, what can you do to counteract that?

Think about someone you could encourage today. What practical steps will you take?

Are you suffering a lack of real life friends? One thing that has helped me is involvement in a local church and even small group. If you aren't connecting with people locally, brainstorm ways you can meet potential friends (play group, school drop-off, reaching out to neighbors, church, etc).

Prayer

Dear Lord,

I know that I need friends in my life. I also need to be a friend to others. Please help me make the time for real-life relationships and to be an encouragement where I can. Bring the people into my life that can encourage me as well. Thank you that you care about all the details in my life.

Amen

Military Marriage

Day 14: Feed the Fish

"A successful marriage requires falling in love many times, always with the same person." -Mignon McLaughlin

We're hitting the age when it seems that many of our contemporaries, including couples who've been together for decades, are quietly divorcing. They've grown apart...they've had long-standing issues...the pressures of military life have proven to be greater than the love that's only a memory now...the kids are grown and they find themselves married to a stranger.

One evening, I was in the kitchen busily prepping dinner in a rush so I could get back to my laptop to finish some editing work.

"Do you want to feed the fish?" my husband asked.

Covered with flour from baking, thinking of all my deadlines, I nodded and wiped off my hands. "Feeding the fish" for us meant, "Will you come be with me a while?"

During our assignment in Hawaii, one of our favorite things to do was walk to the channel behind our house and watch the multi-colored tropical fish surface to snatch at the crumbs we threw. We saw all kinds of fish there: angel fish, clown fish, parrot fish, barracuda, and, several times, baby hammerhead sharks. We took our time, watching the fish and talking. It was a moment to step away from the busyness of life, to do something not necessarily productive, to enjoy nature. As we tossed bread into the water, we reviewed the day, caught up, and reconnected.

When you've been married a long time like we have, it's easy to forget how much those simple moments mean…but to me, they are more important than jewelry or a fancy date. It means my husband still loves me, longs for my company. It is hard for me to "do nothing," but then I remember—it is *something*. This is the most important relationship in my life. I hope that, whatever it means in your own marriage, you'll take time to *feed the fish*.

Every marriage has its challenges, but throw in all the stressors that come with military life, and it's a tricky balancing act. You need to be an independent spouse, able to get along when you're by yourself, yet still make space in your home and heart so that your spouse feels needed when he's there. There are readjustments after deployments, extended family issues, and even, at times, being the only friend the other has. A military marriage can falter under such intensity, so it's best to have your eyes wide open about the challenges so you're not surprised.

Basic Training for Spouses

Staying connected with your spouse requires time and effort, whether or not you have children! If you have a spouse who travels a lot, like mine does, it can be a challenge to maintain life at home and yet make them feel welcomed into family life when they return. Some tips for staying connected:

Find a mutual interest: For us, it's biking, hiking, and…reality TV! (Yes, we're a little nuts.) But when he's on the road, we compare notes on the latest episode of *Survivor* or *The Amazing Race* or discuss the latest antics on *Dance Moms*. (Yes, really.) When we're together, we enjoy exploring new hiking and nature trails together.

Speak well of your spouse: Your spouse's heart should completely trust in you (Proverbs 31). He should know that, when he's absent, you're not complaining about him. You should be able to have that same trust in return!

Pray for your spouse: Though this may not seem like an action, it really is! Praying regularly for your spouse has the benefit of keeping your heart softened. By seeing him through God's eyes, you'll be reminded to lean towards mercy and love without conditions. Pray for your marriage overall and your spouse as an individual, even if you're in the middle of a squabble (especially then!).

Scripture

"And this is my prayer: that your love may abound more and more in knowledge and depth of insight, so that you may be able to discern what is best and may be pure and blameless for the day of Christ, filled with the fruit of righteousness that comes through Jesus Christ—to the glory and praise of God" (Philippians 1:9-11).

"Two people are better off than one, for they can help each other succeed. If one person falls, the other can reach out and help. But someone who falls alone is in real trouble. Likewise, two people lying close together can keep each other warm. But how can one be warm alone?" (Ecclesiastes 4:9-12).

Think About It

What does "feeding the fish" mean for your marriage?

What can you do today to cultivate closeness with your spouse?

Prayer

Dear Lord,

Please help me not to let the challenges of military life come between me and my spouse. Please renew and refresh our relationship, and help us look to you for guidance. Keep my heart turned to my spouse and softened during the difficult times, and let me be an encouragement.

Amen

Day 15: Called to Serve

"Preach the Gospel. Use words if necessary."
-attributed to St. Francis of Assisi

As young marrieds, my husband and I had both been on short-term mission trips with a vision of going into full-time church or missionary work at some point. We figured he would serve his initial military commitment and then we would get on with our real lives. I grew up fascinated by stories of my missionary great-grandparents who served in China, where my grandmother was born in the 1920s. My grandfather was a pastor, as was my father. Our family was deeply involved in the local church and treasured those relationships. The thought of full-time ministry was comfortable and familiar to me, and I envisioned us either moving to another country and settling in as long-term missionaries or perhaps taking on a full-time position at a local church.

At the end of my husband's initial four-year military commitment, we both realized *this* military life was our future. Through repeated assurances of many specific answers to prayers for direction--we knew. It was a time of readjustment, of rethinking our future.

I hadn't really considered that my husband might stay in the military for decades. I didn't suspect that my life would be more that of a tumbleweed, blown from base to base, country to country, rather than one of putting down real roots and forming relationships with people who would know us for many years with shared experiences and a history that tied us to them. I couldn't envision what that would look like or how it would even work.

Each time we'd move to a new base, Steve would go off to his newest job at his newest duty station while I was left to piece together what sort of life I'd have at this location. *Would I have friends? What sort of church would we find? What if the people weren't nice? Would I even have someone to talk to??* The lonely days were punctuated with thoughts of what I perceived as our lack of "ministry" --something we'd felt so called to in those early days of marriage. But I went on, caring for our children, volunteering at church when I could, making a meal here and there for new moms or the sick. It didn't seem like much.

At one point, I said in frustration to my husband, "Are we even making any difference? Does it matter at all?" He was floored. He had a completely different view of things. He'd witnessed so many military marriages shipwreck on the rocks of deployments, frequent moves, and other stressors. Through his job, he stayed aware of family emergencies, domestic abuse, and child neglect/abuse cases that happened within the military community. Our home seemed a safe haven to him; and he believed it was to others, as well. He recognized, acknowledged, and respected a ministry that I didn't even realize I was performing.

If you're like me, you may be wondering what impact you could possibly have on the world around you. Have you ever considered that you do have an impact? That God has placed you right where he wants you? That simply by living your life, day to day, you *are* affecting others?

I can look back now and realize God truly did call us to full-time ministry, but perhaps not in the way I initially expected. In reality, most of us won't ever serve on a foreign mission field, but we are called to serve wherever we are. I hope we can recognize the opportunities right around us: within our families, our neighborhoods, and our communities.

Basic Training for Spouses

Your family life. With the divorce rate in the military at an all-time high, the impact of a healthy marriage (not perfect, mind you) can't be underestimated. Participating in the local church, helping out deployed families, and simply living life together makes an impact. One outlet I've also discovered is the outreach to young troops who may be away from home for the first time, such as meals for dorms/barracks or opening your home to host them during the holidays. Though it may seem simple, your family life can have a huge impact on others.

Your community. If you live on base, which means everyone has job security and there are few elderly people, consider seeking out ministries like working with the homeless or visiting a nursing home in your local area so your children have a wider exposure to all walks of life.

The "least of these." Opening your home to other children can be an unexpected blessing. Dual-military couples might need short-term help with childcare or for you to be an emergency contact when they're deployed or traveling. Perhaps your home could serve as a safe place for kids after school. One of my son's friends stayed with us for a couple of months so he could graduate with his friends when his parents had to transfer before the school year ended.

Your own. Our children are well-acquainted with our shortcomings; there's no way around it! Transparency with our own struggles is so important for our kids so they realize this Christian life is a work in progress, and we are definitely "not there" yet. Early on, we came to the humbling realization that we were raising fellow Christians right in our own home.

The answers that God provided to the desires of our hearts regarding missions were not what we chose initially. Though you may have never had a similar desire to go on a mission trip, I hope you will look around at where God has placed *you* and ask, "Lord, how can I serve where you have me...today?"

Scripture

"Be ready to speak up and tell anyone who asks why you're living the way you are, and always with the utmost courtesy" (1 Peter 3:15, The Message).

"And if anyone gives even a cup of cold water to one of these little ones who is my disciple, truly I tell you, that person will certainly not lose their reward" (Matthew 10:42).

"These commandments that I give you today are to be on your hearts. Impress them on your children. Talk about them when you sit at home and when you walk along the road, when you lie down and when you get up" (Deuteronomy 6: 6, 7).

"In the same way, let your light shine before others, that they may see your good deeds and glorify your Father in heaven" (Matthew 5:16).

Think About It

Has God laid on your heart a specific ministry or desire to serve others?

How can you serve others in the situation you find yourself in right now? Pray to notice the needs around you that you might help to fill. You don't need to wait!

Prayer

Dear Lord,

I pray that you use me where you've placed me right now, whether or not it looks like I'd imagined. Please use me to reach my neighbors, coworkers, and friends with your love. Remind me it's not my job to change anyone, only to shine your light for others.

Amen

Day 16: The Military Didn't Issue a Spouse

"Be kind, for everyone you meet is fighting a hard battle."
–Unknown

Phew, I thought, as intermission was called. I'd made it through the formal part of the dinner. Steve and I were seated at the head table, where he'd acted as the guest speaker for the Airman Leadership School graduation. Proud of him and apparently a little too giddy over making it through the meal without dropping a fork or forcing some other awkward moment, I leaned forward to shake hands with the commanding general...promptly knocking over my water glass with my other wayward hand!

Thankfully, he was a kind person who helped me mop up my mess. I even laughed a little. The picture of the 1950s "typical" white-gloved, genteel military spouse I am most decidedly *not*, and I've learned to laugh at myself as I never know when I might a) trip over a threshold entering a receiving line, b) leave food between my teeth, or c) talk too loudly. My inner klutz always finds a way to shine through! The only comfort I can find in this is that others have told me that my "normalness" has helped them feel more at ease. I will take that!

The longer your spouse is in the military, the greater the likelihood that you'll have the opportunity to attend a military spouses' conference or training, whether it's Key Spouses, commanders or senior enlisted spouses' courses, or something else. The military acknowledges the role that spouses fill and invests time, money, and training into helping us do that well. Thankfully, the days of learning napkin folding and flower arranging seem to be behind us! Courses these days are more focused on real-life scenarios such as deployed family issues, tragedy assistance, and helping new spouses adjust to military life.

There were years that I lamented my lack of time to be involved in volunteering for the military community. Caring for our family, holding down the fort while Steve was gone, and the kids' activities were more than enough of a job for those years. So I never want to put pressure on anyone to volunteer or be more involved than they're comfortable with.

That said, many spouses have admitted to me that they feel an unspoken expectation to be visible or volunteer. Please, take a little bit of unsolicited advice from me: let that go and only do what you want. And if you do desire to be involved? Find a cause that inspires you! Is it supporting deployed families? Volunteering at your child's school? Something else entirely? Through the years, I've served on boards and later been an adviser to spouses' groups, supported unit activities, and helped with booster clubs and organizing meals for new moms. It has just depended on the base, my available time, and how much or little help is needed. You, too, will likely have the opportunity to volunteer in some capacity during your years as a military spouse. It can be so rewarding and the options are endless! But how do you balance that role against your own commitments?

Basic Training for Spouses

Whether you're a new or veteran spouse, you may feel pressure to be involved. Understand that if someone is telling you that you're *required* to volunteer, they're simply wrong. Whatever you choose to do is just that...*your* choice! If you opt to volunteer and help out military families, more power to you! If you don't find yourself with the time right now, that is okay, too. Whatever you choose to do, here are some guidelines that may serve you well.

Be nice. The power of simple kindness is sorely underrated in this era of social media and instant feedback. A smile or kind word can make such a difference to others.

Be yourself. You don't have to change who you are simply because you're a military spouse! The unique qualities and experiences you bring to the table are enough.

Don't gossip. This rarely turns out well. Have a trusted friend or two to vent to, but realize in the small military world, your words may come back to haunt you.

Don't burn yourself out. The saying "How do you get something done? Ask a busy person!" has a ring of truth to it, but it's not necessarily healthy for the busy person. Choose one or two things and do them well. As I mentioned above, one hint on what might be the best place to serve would be the answer to the question, *What are you most passionate about?* By limiting yourself to your strong points, you give others the chance to step up, too.

Take your cues from the military member. Ask your spouse what's important to them. You may be surprised at the answer! The events and activities that are important to my husband are usually much less than what I'd thought I *ought to be doing* (or even what pressure others have brought to bear). At the end of the day, your spouse's opinion is more important than what so-and-so's spouse thinks.

Do what you can and let the rest go. *Permission granted to lay aside unnecessary guilt.* Whether you choose to be involved in your military community a little, a lot, or not at all, make your decision and go on with your life!

Scripture

"Do to others what you'd have them do to you" (Luke 6:31).

"Keep on loving one another as brothers and sisters. Do not forget to show hospitality to strangers, for by so doing some people have shown hospitality to angels without knowing it" (Hebrews 13:1-2).

Think About It

Begin to see your activities as the ministry they are. Such simple things as being available to drop a meal off to a new mom or making a quick phone call or email to check on a deployed spouse may mean more than you realize. What activity can you stop seeing as a "must do" and instead view as a way to show hospitality, an opportunity to honor God through your actions?

Take inventory of your volunteering. It's easy to get caught up in busyness and neglect your own personal and family life ending up replacing the *best* with the *good*. Is there an activity you need to let go?

Prayer

Dear Lord,

I pray that how I choose to spend my time would please you. Give me discernment about what is best for this season of my life. Help me to let go of the things I shouldn't do or don't have time for right now. Give me courage to step up when I need to, and help me learn balance in all things.

Amen

A Life of Transition: Moving with the Military

Day 17: Living in the Pause

"Lead, kindly Light, amid the encircling gloom,

Lead Thou me on!

The night is dark, and I am far from home—

Lead Thou me on!

Keep Thou my feet; I do not ask to see

The distant scene—one step enough for me."

-Cardinal John Henry Newman

Anonymous...raw...lost.

Even though it had been a mere two years since our last military-mandated move, I'd nearly forgotten the feelings that would hit me on leaving a beloved location and slipping in quietly to the next.

We were the new folks...again. Our family's fifth move in six years hit me hard, and some of it probably had to do with the culture shock of returning to U.S. mainland after several years of consecutive overseas assignments. Along with the familiar unfamiliarity of our home country, we all felt the homesickness for places we knew we'd never stay permanently and the now well-known (to us) feeling of life being on hold. As my teenaged daughter and I strolled the streets of our new neighborhood one evening, we imagined aloud how different life would feel in a few months when we'd finally settled in our house and might have found important things like a church, hairdresser, and some friends. She remarked astutely, "It's as if our lives are on 'pause' right now."

I'd bet you understand this feeling. If you also find yourself in that strange transition time following a move, it can seem that everyone else is still going forward (including your spouse who's at a new job and meeting new people) while your own life has come to a standstill.

It's a mixed blessing, this abrupt grinding to a halt of the too-busy life we raced through a few weeks ago. We're forced to stop and reassess everything, whether we like it or not. And what we choose to include in our lives is now a choice, no longer a default.

Embracing life in the pause requires stillness and a willingness to submit myself to God's will. As someone who would rather "do" than be still, these are not natural traits for me! How about you? But I've found that the Lord has used these times of forced change to bring me clarity, teach me to think outside myself, and draw me closer to him.

Basic Training for Spouses

Embracing life in the pause isn't easy. Allow yourself to walk through each step in this process.

Grieve what's lost. Glossing over the challenges of any huge change and referring to it as something our families must simply accept doesn't help anyone. Ultimately, we do eventually accept it because Uncle Sam said so, but allow your family--and yourself--time to grieve leaving beloved friends and places. Being transparent and letting them know you're not immune to the love it/hate it feelings about military life may help them more than you realize.

Be honest. Remember the good times, but be willing to move forward. Maybe you've just left the greatest assignment and said goodbye to the best friend you've ever had. Yes, cherish and maintain those friendships, but don't close yourself off to new experiences. On that note…

Don't compare. It's difficult not to compare what once was to what you seemingly face now. But circumstances are not always what they seem and first impressions can be deceiving. A place you hate on first sight may turn out to be one of your best assignments.

Look at this as a second (or third, or ninth…) chance. Recognize this time as an opportunity to start fresh, to even reinvent yourself. That job you'd learned to dread and the boss who made your life miserable? *Gone!* The difficult neighbor? *Not your problem anymore!* This is also the perfect time to make changes and seriously consider opportunities you've always wanted to pursue.

Lessons are usually better understood through the lens of hindsight, not while you're slogging through difficult circumstances. None of us enjoy saying goodbye to comfortable situations, and the known is preferable to striking out and beginning again. Yet by shifting perspective ever so slightly, "life in the pause" can turn out to be an unexpected gift.

Scripture

"You will keep in perfect peace all who trust in you, all whose thoughts are fixed on you" (Isaiah 26:3, NLT)

"Trust in the Lord with all your heart and lean not on your own understanding; in all your ways submit to him, and he will make your paths straight" (Proverbs 3: 5,6).

Think About It

If you find yourself living "in the pause" right now, choose an encouraging verse and write it at the end of this reading to remind your heart of God's goodness.

What is the most difficult part of transition for you? Is it the goodbyes, making new friends, or something else?

Prayer

Dear Lord

I know you've brought me here for a reason. Though life may seem to be at a standstill, remind me that you are always moving, always working, even if it's in the unseen reaches of my own heart.

Amen

Day 18: Lessons from Living Out of a Suitcase

"Worrying is carrying tomorrow's load with today's strength--carrying two days at once. It is moving into tomorrow ahead of time. Worrying doesn't empty tomorrow of its sorrow, it empties today of its strength." -Corrie Ten Boom, *The Hiding Place*

Military spouses know that "urge to purge" that comes from having orders in hand. Whether or not you're facing a PCS anytime soon, I bet you know the drill: organizing piles and sorting out closets in preparation for another move. Some moves require a family to live out of suitcases for weeks or even months as they wait for housing to become available, or move overseas while household goods wend their way across the ocean.

Our family's longest span of living out of our suitcases lasted nearly five months as we relocated from a tiny island in the Western Pacific back to the U.S. We were told that it would be a few weeks to wait for the new base housing to open while we lived in temporary lodging…which ended up up stretching into several months!

In spite of the inconvenience, I look back on that time of forced family closeness with fond memories. We became masters at keeping four active kids occupied with few belongings in a small space! Playing catch with a nerf ball in our billeting room (I'm sure the neighbors loved us), daily walks to the library to swap out videos, loads and loads of card games, and rediscovering cable TV cooking shows after our time overseas were some pastimes. I also found out that we needed much less to live on than we thought.

As far as household items go, I tend to overestimate the amount of "stuff" I need for daily life—stuff that ends up hindering, rather than helping. One unforeseen benefit that has come from moving so often is that I've been forced to deny my natural hoarding tendencies. The items we end up moving from household to household are things needed for daily life or ones that we truly value for sentimental reasons. Family antiques, handwritten treasures from my children, photo-filled scrapbooks, a remembrance book crafted by my grandmother's hands, gifts that Steve has brought back from his travels, and unique items collected from the Pacific to Europe make the list. Each one has some meaning attached to it, some known only to our family.

Easier to leave behind are what one would consider junk...old hangers and tired plasticware or clothing that fit me a few years ago that I'm just "ten pounds away" from fitting back into. The things which end up in the garbage bin are the items easily replaced or worn out.

Things that hinder, rather than help.

Basic Training for Spouses

How much *junk*, spiritually and emotionally speaking, do we insist on dragging around in our hearts? What emotions and memories do we waste our precious time on: metaphorically pulling them out of their hiding spots, folding each one carefully or arranging until they are just so, organizing into similar piles, and then gently placing them back into their specially reserved spot in our souls? The problem is, these are things that don't warrant such consideration or time spent: worry over the future, regrets, bitterness, preconceived notions, wrong judgments....*things that only hinder, never help.*

It's probably time to do a soul purge and leave those items behind as easily as we chunk the old Tupperware into the trash. They do just about as much good! How much better for us to replace those old things with forgiveness, sympathy, understanding, and a willingness to forget?

"Packing light" takes on new meaning for me when I consider the baggage I so often choose to tote around so needlessly in my soul.

Scripture

"….let us throw off everything that hinders and the sin that so easily entangles, and let us run with perseverance the race marked out for us." (Hebrews 12:1)

"See, I am doing a new thing!

Now it springs up; do you not perceive it?

I am making a way in the wilderness

and streams in the wasteland" (Isaiah 43:19).

"...I have come that they may have life, and have it to the full" (John 10:10)

Think About It

Are there things in your life that no longer belong or warrant space? What physical items are clogging up your house?

Spiritually speaking, what baggage can you eliminate? What items or even people and situations are you grasping tightly and resisting giving over to the Lord? Has he convicted you to let some*one* or some*thing* go?

Sometimes letting go of baggage may require making things right or apologizing to another person. Is there someone in your life you need to speak with in order to move on to a new phase?

Prayer

Dear Lord,

I need your help every day to let go of the things I know I shouldn't hold on to. Give me strength to stop clinging to old habits and bitterness. Help me remember to pack lightly, whether it's in this physical life or the things I choose to cherish in my soul. Thank you that you are indeed doing a 'new thing' in my life each day.

Amen

Day 19: Embracing Where You Live

"Begin challenging your own assumptions. Your assumptions are your windows on the world. Scrub them off every once in a while, or the light won't come in." -Alan Alda

"I could live anywhere but _____."

"If my spouse gets an overseas assignment, I'm *not* going."

I'm a little mystified when I hear statements like the above. While each family's answer to the question "Should I stay or should I go?" is personal, ours has benefited from the opportunities we've had to travel and experience places we might not have visited otherwise. We've skied in the Alps, snorkeled the Great Barrier Reef, strolled through the streets of Rome, London, and Paris, and lived on two tropical islands. Our kids traveled to Greece, Poland, Lithuania, and other countries for mission trips, youth retreats, and sports tournaments when we were stationed in Germany.

A little closer to home in the U.S., we've lived within view of the Capitol building in D.C., held onto our hats while skimming across the Everglades in a fan boat, shoveled feet of snow in North Dakota, and strolled through the coolness of the giant redwood forests. From my desk in Hawaii, I often stopped to watch submarines and ships slip into the Pearl Harbor channel. As a young girl growing up in the desert southwest, these were places I'd only read about, much less thought I'd ever see in person, and I'm so grateful for where this military life has taken us.

While moving on to a new assignment isn't ever easy, I hope you will begin to view military life as the adventure it can be!

Basic Training for Spouses

Give yourself time and grace to get used to the new location. Whether it's a new state or a new country, culture shock is real, even down to whether you call your drink "soda" or "pop"! Begin exploring little by little and take your time to adjust. And then...

Get out there! We've all run across people who maintain they hate a location, yet never took the time to visit even the basic tourist locations. If you live on post/base overseas, it can be tempting to stay in that safe little military cocoon. Remind yourself that some people would give anything to travel! You may be thousands of miles from "home," but guess what? You're living someone else's dream! Enlist a friend with an adventurous spirit to be your sightseeing buddy.

Explore where you live. What if you feel stuck in Smalltown, USA? Make the most of it! A friend once suggested taking a map and drawing a 25-50 mile radius around where you live. Then, determine to hit every tourist or landmark spot in that area. (You can do this on the map app on your phone!) Branch out further once you've done that. When we lived in North Dakota (admittedly not a typical tourist destination), we hunted for antiques at estate sales in giant old barns, picked strawberries from the fields of a local grower, snapped photos by huge sunflower fields, and drove to the Badlands on the other side of the state. No matter where you are, I'm pretty sure you can find something new to do.

Buddy up with the locals. Whether U.S. or overseas, these are the folks who will point you to the hole-in-the wall food joints, best shopping, and areas to avoid. Make the most of these local experts. People are usually proud of where they live and happily share their knowledge when asked. You might also make a new friend!

What if I just hate my location? It would be the rare location that is *all bad*. Does this sound too chipper to be true? Sure, there are challenges. No one is head over heels in love with every assignment, and we've all counted down the days till we leave some places. Try to find a bright side-- whether it's a nature trail, sunny beach, or new store--so you're not constantly focused on the negative.

For instance, when we left Hawaii to return to the mainland, it took a *lot* of effort for me to find the bright side. Here's what I came up with: closer proximity to family, lower cost of living, and even rediscovering some fast food places we'd missed!

Scripture

"Give thanks in all circumstances; for this is God's will for you in Christ Jesus" (1 Thessalonians 5:18).

"Do not be anxious about anything, but in every situation, by prayer and petition, with thanksgiving, present your requests to God. And the peace of God, which transcends all understanding, will guard your hearts and your minds in Christ Jesus" (Philippians 4:6-7).

"And we know that for those who love God all things work together for good, for those who are called according to his purpose" (Romans 8:28, ESV).

Think About It

What steps can you take to "embrace where you live" today?

Do a quick search and list three places you haven't visited yet in your local area and make concrete plans to explore them!

Is someone you know struggling with a new location? Is there a way you can help them adjust?

Prayer

Dear Lord,

I find myself not in control of my circumstances. Help me to embrace Your leading in where you've placed me and trust that you only have my good in mind. Give me a spirit of gratitude and help me see what's around me with new eyes. Thank you for courage to venture out beyond my comfort zone and to notice others who might be struggling, too.

Amen

Separations: Dealing with TDYs and Deployments

Day 20: Goodbye, Again

"You have to say goodbye if you want to say hello again."
-My grandmother

I wiped the sweat out of my eyes and pushed the mower through the thick Florida grass. Glancing up at the front window, I spotted my nine-year-old perched on the back of the couch, giving me a thumbs-up and a proud smile at being in charge of letting me know when the baby woke up from her nap. I waved at him and hurried to finish the yard work.

This was my life with four young children while my husband left for an extended TDY, rushing through tasks that he and I would normally split when he was home. My oldest was not quite old enough to take on chores like lawn mowing, but he could sit in the living room, listen to the baby monitor, and let me know everything was a-ok. My kids are older now—three of them grown—and I no longer look anxiously at the window to see if little ones need me. But I honestly believe there's no good age for kids to be without a parent. Toddlers or teens, it's hard.

I've heard military counselors remark that having a loved one deployed is akin to dealing with a long-term illness or family trauma. It's an incredible, ongoing stress. There are times when you simply can't be cheered up, and a light-hearted moment doesn't help you shake off the deployment blues.

What are you supposed to do when you've had it up to *here* with being alone, with carrying the weight of the family on your shoulders, with worry over how it's affecting your children, with thinking you simply cannot do this *one. more. blasted. day?*

There aren't any easy answers. I've sat at countless soccer games and cheered my kids on alone, argued with an auto mechanic about the cost of repairs (while my mind screamed, *I shouldn't have to deal with this--my husband is the car guy!*), cried irrationally over little challenges I'd normally let roll off my shoulders, and wrestled through more sleepless nights than I can count.

When I go through long periods of separation from my husband, I often don't realize how tense I am until he returns home and a near physical weight drops from my shoulders. I find myself exhausted for a few days, needing more sleep, and feeling as though I'm recovering from an illness. Other spouses concur that they've experienced this, too.

During our long goodbyes, I've snapped when I should have bent and questioned when I ought to have trusted. I'm thankful that God has promised new mercies for each day...and that he meets me right at my moment of need. He will meet you, too.

Basic Training for Spouses

It's good to recognize our limitations, because it's at the intersection of exhaustion and desperation that God promises to be with us.

"...then he told me,

My grace is enough; it's all you need.

My strength comes into its own in your weakness.

Once I heard that, I was glad to let it happen. I quit focusing on the handicap and began appreciating the gift. It

was a case of Christ's strength moving in on my weakness.
Now I take limitations in stride, and with good cheer, these
limitations that cut me down to size—abuse, accidents,
opposition, bad breaks. I just let Christ take over! And so
the weaker I get, the stronger I become" (2 Corinthians
12:10, The Message).

Scripture

"Have I not commanded you? Be strong and courageous.
Do not be afraid; do not be discouraged, for the Lord your
God will be with you wherever you go" (Joshua 1:9).

"I remain confident of this:

I will see the goodness of the Lord

  in the land of the living" (Psalms 27:13).

Think About It

What's your biggest area of weakness when you're
separated from your spouse? Is it fear, anger, resentment?
Write it out.

Now, in what specific ways can you trust God with each of
those things? For instance, when I used to fret over how
military separations would affect my children, I learned to
pray, "Lord, YOU knew about this beforehand. I trust
YOU to see my child through this." Reminding myself of
God's providence in times of unwanted separation has
been important for me. You may have a different worry
entirely-- take a moment to remind yourself of how God
worked through that circumstance in the past.

Prayer

Dear Lord,

Even on the days I seem to be coping fine with separations, I am struggling--with loneliness, with frustration, with fear, with anger. Remind me of your care and fill my heart with the peace that comes from trusting you with my future. Help me remember that you care for each member of my family and are always working. I pray for your protective hand over my spouse as we're separated. Thank you that, even in my weakness, you are strong.

Amen

Day 21: The Purple Wig

"If we couldn't laugh, we would all go insane." -Robert Frost

"*What* does Mom have on her head?" shrieked my daughter.

I turned to look at my children, flipped my purple locks over my shoulder, and continued on to the laundry room as if nothing were amiss. Peals of laughter followed, and my kids scrambled after me, begging to try the wig on for themselves. Even more surprising about this little scene? My husband had left days earlier for a six-month deployment. But for a few precious moments, laughter helped us forget the worry and anxiety.

The previous week, we'd all moped around with that empty feeling that family members of the recently deployed know all too well. It didn't seem as if we could give ourselves permission to think about anything but their Dad and what was going on *over there*. The months ahead without him stretched out endlessly.

I had been unsure about how to get us out of this funk, and thought and prayed about what to do. One evening, while driving my children to (yet) another activity, I passed a party store. An idea began to form, and I made time to get back to that store alone. I bought cheap wigs, funny glasses, and even a big nose and mustache. I hid my stash when we got home and could not wait to ambush my kids.

The next day, with a purple foil wig atop my head, I nonchalantly strolled through the living room while toting a laundry basket. My children, sprawled on the floor watching TV, didn't react. The funniest part? I had to make three passes through the room before anyone noticed!

Over the following months, I would pull another wig or pair of goofy glasses out of my bag at random times and turn up unexpectedly with my newest get-up. It became quite a game with the kids trying to guess what would come next, and me having an absolute blast surprising them. (Though I don't suggest answering the doorbell in a pair of googly-eyed glasses--don't ask.) It became a special, unexpected memory of that time.

Our family has now been through many separations and deployments and we've learned a few things about getting through the time. You may feel guilt at having "fun" while your spouse is gone, but my husband has shared that he likes to think of his family still enjoying normal life and making memories. I have a feeling this might be true for others, as well.

Basic Training for Spouses

How to add some moments of lightness to a trying time like a deployment?

Have a themed day. Some ideas: pajama days, ice cream for dinner, or all-day-movie days. Along with the pajama theme, eat only breakfast foods for all your meals that day. Your kids will think you're the cooliest!

Do something surprising. Interrupt the humdrum, daily routine with a treat now and then, even if it's something as simple as stopping at the park or renting a movie and staying up later than usual. And you can bet that walking through the room with a crazy wig on your head will surprise your kids and get them laughing! It's the unexpected moments here and there that can lift all of your spirits. Once you get in the habit, you'll begin to look for your own fun ways to surprise your children. It doesn't have to be anything fancy--just surprising!

Refresh yourself, too. What relaxes or reinvigorates you? Is it a long drive, going to the movies, or attending church regularly? Even when you don't feel like it, try to continue to do those things. Your spirit needs refreshing, too.

Long deployments and TDYs can become overwhelming, especially if you start to think of it as one long, dreaded block of time. Plan to break it up with creative ideas to help lighten up your family during the months of separation. It might even include a purple wig!

Scripture

"A cheerful heart is good medicine, but a crushed spirit dries up the bones" (Proverbs 17:22).

"He will yet fill your mouth with laughter and your lips with shouts of joy" (Job 8:21).

Think About It

List a fun activity you can do with your family this week.

If you're not currently going through a military-driven separation, perhaps you're in a place to help someone else who is. Brainstorm some ways of reaching out to those around you who obviously could use a respite or a lighter moment. Surely you know a family with special needs, an elderly person, or someone struggling with an illness or other challenge who could use a kind word or practical help!

Prayer

Dear Lord,

Thank you for the reminder that a merry heart can be a welcome respite during times of stress. Help me to notice the little ways that I can help lift the spirits of my family. Thank you for your creativity in how you deal with us, your children.

Amen

Day 22: When My Heart Is Overwhelmed

"Faith is taking the first step even when you can't see the whole staircase." -Dr. Martin Luther King, Jr.

"Kandahar Air Field is currently undergoing a ground assault."

As I drove home from the commissary one spring afternoon, the words crackled over the American Forces Network radio station like the echoes from my worst nightmare. Pulling over, I gripped the steering wheel as my two younger children and I sat in stunned silence, listening to the news report. *Kandahar!* That's where my husband—their father—was currently serving in Afghanistan. I'd attempted to shield our four children from the bad news constantly playing out in the media, but this was not a dream--and we were all too awake.

Earlier that day, while taking a short nap, I'd dreamed that my husband was home with us again. I saw him standing in the doorway in his full dress uniform, smiling at me wordlessly. He looked so handsome, and I couldn't believe he was back early. Sitting up to start toward the door, he disappeared. Waking suddenly, I wondered what the dream meant, glanced at the clock, and registered the time—late afternoon in Germany where we were stationed. Unsure of any meaning other than that I was missing him after nine months of being apart, I lifted up a prayer for his safety and set about my errands on base, continuing to pray for him frequently.

Now, thinking of the dream earlier and this startling news, I couldn't help but wonder if God was gently preparing me for the worst.

I don't recall much about the rest of the drive home, other than the shocked silence and the sick feeling in my stomach. I listened as my daughter told the rest of the children the news, but felt removed--as if I were observing someone else's life.

All I could think was, *This can't be happening. We only have a few months left before he comes home.*

During that long evening of waiting for word, Psalm 37 came to my mind.

"The Lord makes firm the steps of the one who delights in him; though he may stumble, he will not fall, for the Lord upholds him with his hand." (Psalm 37:23, 24).

Some of the most agonizing hours of my life passed that night as I sat alone, praying and waiting. Steve was deployed in a fairly austere area, so we'd felt fortunate to send him daily e-mails and receive calls from him each week. But it had now been silent for nearly 24 hours. I turned off the news and stopped checking the internet, as I couldn't bear to hear the story of the attack playing out repeatedly. And still…no word from him.

Finally, in the early morning hours, the phone rang. The connection was terrible, the call brief, but my husband's voice had never sounded so wonderful! He said casually, "So you may have heard about an attack…"

Days later, he confirmed the attack had happened about the time I'd had the dream which prompted me to pray for him. I don't believe in coincidence and I know that God led me to pray for him and the others at his base at just the right moment.

Basic Training for Spouses

Trusting when you don't know the end result. Though I didn't know the outcome, I knew that no matter what happened, God would walk through it with us. He would not leave us alone. Even if we stumbled, he was there. He hadn't promised that we'd never face trouble. But *he had promised to uphold us.* We'd lost a beloved family friend to a premature death just months before, and the reality of death was clear to all of us. We knew that we weren't guaranteed what we wanted and that bad things happen to good people, yet we believed that if the worst did happen, God would carry us.

The prayer that never fails. Knowing that God prepared me for whatever was to come, I'm truly grateful for his mercy in dealing with our family. I've found, however, that it's nearly impossible to prepare for unknown scenarios beyond simply trusting God's will. Jan Karon's beloved character from the *Mitford* series, Father Tim, calls the words from the Lord's Prayer, "Thy will be done," **the prayer that never fails.** You might find this to be true, as well.

Scripture

"He who dwells in the shelter of the Most High will abide in the shadow of the Almighty. I will say to the Lord, "My refuge and my fortress, my God, in whom I trust!" (Psalm 91:1-2, ESV).

"Be strong and courageous. Do not be afraid or terrified because of them, for the LORD your God goes with you;

he will never leave you nor forsake you" (Deuteronomy 31:6).

"Hear my cry, O God; listen to my prayer. From the ends of the earth I call to you, I call as my heart grows faint; lead me to the rock that is higher than I. For you have been my refuge, a strong tower against the foe" (Psalm 61:1-3).

Think About It

Is there anything you have difficulty saying about, "Not MY will, but yours, God"?

Write out and consider memorizing your favorite Scripture for when you face times of trouble.

Prayer

Dear Lord,

I don't know the future, but you do. Help me to trust in your unfailing love, no matter what happens. Thank you that I can trust you to know what's best for me. Thank you for upholding me, through good times and bad.

Amen

Day 23: Hello, Again

"The things you take for granted, someone else is praying for."
– Anonymous

I even missed the sound of his snoring. Waking up at night to a
deadly quiet room without the sounds of my husband
nearby was one of the hardest things to get used to during
his deployments. I never felt more alone than I did at 3 a.m.

When homecoming day arrives, emotions tend to run high.
You will probably experience a honeymoon period at the
gladness of being together again. I hope you do! But you
may also have some struggles during the period known as
reintegration--those days, weeks, and even months after a
deployment or long separation.

You've waited for this day...you missed each other so...you
couldn't wait to feel his arms around you again. But after
several days back together, everything seems a little..*off.* You
didn't expect the growing pains that would go along with
the post-deployment phase. You feel like a stranger is living
with you. He's wondering about decisions you made while
he's been away. You think he seems distant and wonder
why something like socks left on the floor causes a
disproportionate amount of irritation to rise up in you.

So then you question yourself. After all, what kind of
person wouldn't be grateful that her spouse is back after
months apart? Why are these little things so annoying? You
wonder, *what is wrong with me?*

How do you rebuild a life after deployment?

Basic Training for Spouses

Name the feelings. You may feel confused, misunderstood, sad that things aren't going the way you'd envisioned. You may feel lonely, which may not make sense to you since your spouse is sitting five feet away. You may feel guilty that your spouse came home and others didn't. You may wonder why you feel so tired or why the separation was so difficult when it was "just" a separation. Don't try to understand the feelings right now, just acknowledge them.

Know that it's common. After the honeymoon period, there will likely be some tense times of readjustment. From other spouses I've spoken to and military spouse literature (see resource appendix), it's a comfort to know that these feelings are overwhelmingly common. He may question why you made a certain decision. You may wonder why he's not more affectionate. Work through these issues together--honestly.

Walk a mile in their shoes. This goes both ways. In the days leading up to our last big homecoming, my husband and I discussed at length the reintegration issues we'd dealt with in the past and what we could expect. By then, he'd been in the Air Force over 20 years, so we felt like we had a handle on it. Surprise! We still went through some tough times even though our eyes were wide open to the issues. One thing that helped was for each of us to step back and attempt to see things from the other's point of view. Could I understand everything he'd been through? No, but I could think about how it would feel to be apart from my family for a year. Could he make sense of why I did a certain thing when he might have chosen differently? Not always, but he could try to imagine what it would feel like to function as a virtual single parent for that length of time. Which leads me to...

It's not a contest. Be wary of playing the "I had it tougher than you" game. No one wins. These forced separations are hard on everyone. Now is not the time to compare. Arguing over who had it worse only divides and causes resentment. Remember that you're on the same team.

Be honest moving forward. After you've each named what you're feeling, extended grace, and talked through your concerns, be honest. Are you able to walk through the issues of reintegration together? Or should you seek out the help of a trusted counselor, chaplain, or friend? Make use of resources as you navigate these first months becoming a family again.

Neither of you will be the same. You've both changed; it's inevitable. Pray for patience and generosity as you move forward to the new chapter of your lives. Know that if you can work through these days, an even better and stronger marriage is just ahead.

Scripture

"But the Lord is faithful, and he will strengthen and protect you from the evil one" (2 Thessalonians 3:3).

"And this is my prayer: that your love may abound more and more in knowledge and depth of insight, so that you may be able to discern what is best and may be pure and blameless for the day of Christ, filled with the fruit of righteousness that comes through Jesus Christ--to the glory and praise of God" (Philippians 1:9,10).

Think About It

If you've been apart for a long period of time, you may need to have a time of getting to know each other again. What are some special outings or date nights you could plan? (Maybe it's just staying in and ordering pizza!)

I was actually thankful to hear the sound of my husband snoring nearby again after his last deployment. Make a list of what you're thankful for and focus on those when tensions rise or you feel irritated over seemingly little things.

Prayer

Dear Lord,

I am thankful that you have brought my partner safely back to me. I can't pretend to know what he's been through. Please bring him healing and peace and help us remember our love for each other as we move forward into the next part of our lives. We both need your grace.

Amen

Note: Please see the Resources section for more information and help with deployment issues.

Day 24: Together Yet Apart

"There is no more lovely, friendly or charming relationship, communion or company, than a good marriage." -Martin Luther

My grandfather, who had a fabulous memory and amazing wit before his mind was touched by Alzheimer's, recited the whole of 1 Corinthians 13 at our wedding. I'd heard the verses before, but as the well-known words rolled past me...*Love is patient, love is kind, love does not envy, it does not boast*...I realized the enormity of what we were about to undertake and how it was very likely that neither of were prepared for such lofty promises. It would require a divine intervention to join two such seemingly different people. I'm glad God is still in the business of working miracles.

While we've been through numerous deployments and separations, more recently over the past several years my husband's job includes frequent TDYs ('temporary duty' in Air Force lingo) and many months have seen us apart more than we're together. When these sorts of trips stretch on one after the other, I slip into a routine of being alone: eating odd things at odd hours, working late, being off the schedule we normally have when he's here.

I daresay the same is true for him--being on the road constantly is not conducive to a typical home routine. It's not what either of us would prefer, but what we have to deal with. But let me tell you, hearing his voice on the phone saying "Hi, darlin'" still gives me butterflies all these years since those two young people stood at the altar. Maybe the frequent separations are good for at least one thing--I don't take him for granted! Still, it can be so easy to get caught up in dealing with the busyness of kids' routines and my own work that I have little left to give.

It's important to cultivate our marriage, whether we're physically together or not, and while challenging, it's honestly the little things that can make or break a marriage.

How do we stay connected while dealing with being apart?

Basic Training for Spouses

Simple things matter. A quick call or text letting my husband know I'm thinking of and missing him means a lot. Even a kissy face emoji works in a pinch!

How was your day? I read a survey recently that said couples who ask each other about their day on a regular basis have a higher marriage success rate than couples who don't. Why? My theory is that it shows they are thinking of the other person and are truly interested in what happens to them.

Handwritten notes. Tucking sweet notes into his luggage makes for a nice surprise. On the flip side, when my husband leaves for a trip earlier than I'm awake, a quick kiss on the forehead and a note waiting for me by the coffeepot makes my whole day.

A running email or text. Often, my husband is caught up in briefings and meetings requiring security clearance, which means no access to texting or personal email for hours. Still, I will send him little notes of what's going on here at home. I once asked him if it was annoying to get this continual stream of messages from me. He said, "No, I like it!" It helps him feel connected even when he's not here. And let's be honest--I usually have a lot more words on any given day than he does, so it helps *me* feel connected to think I'm still filling him in on the goings-on.

Talk about him. Don't let your spouse be "out of sight, out of mind." He's still a part of your life. whether at home or not. One of my husband's colleagues mentioned once in passing how much Steve bragged about me and the kids. I was floored! My seemingly reticent husband? I walked around with the biggest grin for days after hearing that. Uplifting your spouse even when they're absent has a powerful effect--on you and those around you.

Scripture

"Love is very patient and kind, never jealous or envious, never boastful or proud, never haughty or selfish or rude. Love does not demand its own way. It is not irritable or touchy. It does not hold grudges and will hardly even notice when others do it wrong. It is never glad about injustice, but rejoices whenever truth wins out. If you love someone, you will be loyal to him no matter what the cost. You will always believe in him, always expect the best of him, and always stand your ground in defending him" (1 Corinthians 13:4-7, TLB).

"So the Lord God caused a deep sleep to fall upon the man, and while he slept took one of his ribs and closed up its place with flesh. And the rib that the Lord God had taken from the man he made into a woman and brought her to the man. Then the man said, "This at last is bone of my bones and flesh of my flesh; she shall be called Woman, because she was taken out of Man." Therefore a man shall leave his father and his mother and hold fast to his wife, and they shall become one flesh" (Genesis 2:21-25, ESV).

"'Haven't you read," he replied, "that at the beginning the Creator 'made them male and female,' and said, 'For this reason a man will leave his father and mother and be united to his wife, and the two will become one flesh.' So they are no longer two, but one flesh. Therefore what God has joined together, let no one separate"' (Matthew 19:4-6).

Think About It

If you and your spouse are apart right now, in what ways can you stay more connected?

Do you find it difficult to express appreciation to your spouse? What steps can you take to help that?

It is easy to focus on negatives. Write down several things that you're thankful for about your spouse today.

Prayer

Dear Lord,

I know you designed marriage and that it is a good thing for me. Help me cling to my spouse above all others and look for creative ways to express my love and let him know he's in my thoughts.

Amen

Military Families and Kids

Day 25: Lessons from My Military Kids

"We spent our entire childhoods in the service of our country, and no one even knew we were there." -Pat Conroy

It's a running joke in our family about the many natural disasters we've been through: earthquakes, hurricanes, blizzards. No matter where we're stationed, it seems we manage to find ourselves in some sort of record breaking blizzard or the flood of the century. During our time in Guam, we went through two major typhoons within one week. This meant several weeks with no power or running water while we waited for services to be restored to the island. I recall moldy furniture and washing out our toddler's clothes with bottled water, using a Lego table as a washboard. The kids remember the privilege of eating dinner at the chow hall, the delight of wearing the same clothes several days' running (*ewww*), and the moment when the lights came on. For the longest time after our power was restored, our four-year-old would accompany the switched-on lights with clapping her chubby hands and gleefully squealing, "Wights on!!"

One day, while watching a TV special on "Military Brats" (I know many of us don't care for the term, but for good or bad, it's stuck and you all know who I'm talking about: the children of a military member), I was struck by the interviews with the now-adult brats and the issues they'd struggled with including feelings of rootlessness, struggles maintaining long-term relationships, and substance abuse. It was daunting to think this could be the outcome for our four children. My then twelve-year-old sat with me while I babbled how sorry I was that they had to move so much—that their dad was deployed AGAIN—that I was just so sorry for the whole darned thing. Her older siblings joined us.

"Mom, it's ok. Really."

I blinked back the tears, and took a look at my children as they assured me. They *were* ok. There were struggles, but they all agreed they wouldn't trade their lives for anything.

Basic Training for Spouses

I learned something that day. Studies aside, my kids (three of them now adults) really were—and *are*—ok. I've talked to other grown military brats who view their childhood as an asset. They're confident, cultured, and well-rounded. The world is a different place than it was for the "brats" interviewed on that show, most of whom grew up during the Vietnam era and the 80's. Moving to a new city is more common in today's culture than it used to be. Social media has made it easier than ever to keep in touch with old friends than it was even five years ago.

I'm not sugarcoating the difficulties and stress that military life places on our children, but I discovered that my kids seem to have the ability to focus on the positive. They've taught me so many lessons about life and faith without even knowing it. What would you add to this list?

Flexibility: Their ability to adapt to whatever situation we're in is amazing. My kids have a flexibility about life that I am still learning.

Resiliency: "Resiliency" has been a catchphrase for the military for some time. But when I look at my kids, I can't help but think of them as *resilient*. They've had quite a few challenges packed into their short lives and they've managed it with grace. They're adaptable and bounce back like nobody's business.

Find fun where you can: Once the movers leave, a tradition for my kids is some sort of indoor (forbidden when pictures and knick-knacks are present) ball game. The large empty rooms seem to invite a little silliness. As soon as the moving van pulls away, I expect to hear laughter ringing from an empty room. And if my husband's home, he's right in the middle of it!

Everyone is a potential friend: They've lived all over the world and have an interesting assortment of friends. If you talk about racism, they can't comprehend why anyone would discriminate based on skin color—or any other factor, for that matter. They understand what makes a true friend.

Embrace life: "YOLO" (You Only Live Once)—why do I feel a military kid could've coined that phrase? They take both big and small risks with gusto! I've watched my kids extend the vulnerable hand of friendship to someone they barely know and learn how to ski on a tall mountain in the Alps. I submit that both acts take equal amounts of bravery.

The world is an amazing place: Our youngest was better traveled at age 10 than I was at 20. When I find myself holding back, I try to look at the world through my kids' eyes. There is always something new to be discovered, places to explore, friends to make, and chocolate to be eaten.

Scripture

"He called a little child to him, and placed the child among them. And he said: 'Truly I tell you, unless you change and become like little children, you will never enter the kingdom of heaven' " (Matthew 18:2).

"If you, then, though you are evil, know how to give good gifts to your children, how much more will your Father in heaven give good gifts to those who ask him!" (Matthew 7:11).

Think About It

What lessons about life have you learned from your kids?

Our kids often teach us by example. That makes me think about my own actions and how they're affecting others around me. Though it can be hard to face, are there areas in your own life that could be a better example to your family and others?

Prayer

Dear Lord,

Thank you for the children you've entrusted me with. Give me a soft heart towards the struggles that they face, even if I can't understand them completely. Help me to be teachable and to realize that I can learn some of life's greatest lessons through my own children. Be with them through all of the unique challenges they face as military kids, and remind them daily of your love.

Amen

Day 26: Solo Parenting

"Parenting: if you're not tired, you're not doing it right!"
-Unknown

I did not sign up for this. That was the thought racing through my mind as I heard the news.

Though our family had already weathered multiple separations and long deployments, I still wasn't prepared for the news that Steve would be deploying for a year--and leaving in a matter of weeks. Even worse? He'd miss our oldest son's entire senior year. The whole. Flippin'. Year.

It's one thing to boldly declare hypothetically: "We will do whatever duty requires of us," but another when you're suddenly faced with losing what you thought was going to be, and what you'd planned and counted on. I'm not ashamed to admit that, though I do manage to buck up and cope with life when the moment of separation comes, there are times that I say, "Enough, God! Haven't we sacrificed enough already?!"

Perhaps you're familiar with the story of Bethany Hamilton. At the age of 13, while surfing in Kauai, Bethany lost her arm in a shark attack. Faced with devastating loss and a complete life change, Bethany not only survived and recovered, but went on to a career as a professional surfer—with one arm. She is a young woman of amazing faith who travels the globe and is very outspoken about her Christian faith. I've been so encouraged by her story. In her words:

> "It helps to know that even when you don't have a
> clue why something has happened in your life,

someone up there has a master plan and is watching you. It's a tremendous relief to be able to put your trust in God and take the burden off your shoulders." 3

Basic Training for Spouses

What does a traumatic and life changing event like the loss of an arm through a shark attack have to do with the "solo" parenting that often ends up being a recurring theme as a military spouse? While I haven't been through anything as traumatic as Bethany Hamilton has, when faced with unwanted transitions in my own life, I can remind myself that *this same God* who has watched over, guided, and inspired Bethany is also looking out for me.

It's tempting to think that we're the only ones who've faced such an experience. Perhaps we even entertain the thought that this circumstance right here is *the one thing* we simply can't do.

It's a good time for this reminder: **God is not surprised.** There is no circumstance, no trial, no *anything* that he can't handle.

That's all well and good, you might be thinking, *but you don't know how things are going for **me**. My kids are driving me bonkers, my washer overflowed, the dog escaped from the yard again, and all I can think about is a nap.*

It's easy to affirm our faith in the Lord and his goodness when life is cruising along. But it's more difficult to trust in his goodness toward us as we face another sleepless night because of worry over our spouse in a war zone. It's not easy to trust in a master plan when faced with another holiday season, birthday, or milestone without your loved one. It's hard to trust when you feel you're doing an inadequate job as you tackle parenting by yourself--*again.*

It's not easy to trust when you see the toll that repeated separations take on your kids. It doesn't help when others say things like, "You knew what you were getting into when you married someone in the military." (!!)

The days can be long and the loneliness deafening. In those moments, it can be difficult to focus on God's faithfulness, and not on the overwhelming burden of temporary circumstances. I find that, at times like that, I cannot take one day or even one hour at a time; it truly becomes a minute-by-minute thing. And God meets me there. Yes, he does.

Scripture

"For I know the plans I have for you," declares the Lord, "plans to prosper you and not to harm you, plans to give you hope and a future" (Jeremiah 29:11).

"Do you not know?

   Have you not heard?

The Lord is the everlasting God,

   the Creator of the ends of the earth.

He will not grow tired or weary,

   and his understanding no one can fathom" (Isaiah 40:28).

"God is our refuge and strength, an ever-present help in trouble. Therefore we will not fear, though the earth give way and the mountains fall into the heart of the sea, though its waters roar and foam and the mountains quake with their surging" (Psalms 46:1-3).

"We can rejoice, too, when we run into problems and trials, for we know that they help us develop endurance" (Romans 5:3, NLT).

Think About It

List the specific areas you're struggling with as you parent alone.

Now, ask God's help to find creative ways to solve some of these challenges. (For instance hiring a sitter once a week so you can get out alone, trading off playdates with a friend, earlier bedtimes for all, etc.)

Is there something you can do today to encourage your heart in this lonely time (coffee with a friend, taking a child on a lunch 'date'--just you and them, time alone)?

What is the one time or circumstance where you find it most difficult to trust God? You might as well admit it, since God already knows!

Prayer

Dear Lord,

Please help me to take my eyes off the temporary today, even in the midst of this difficult time. Help me remember how you've taken care of our family in the past and remind me that you won't stop now. Thank you for strengthening me when I'm weary, and for filling in those spots where I feel I'm failing with my kids. Thank you for being a loving Father to my children.

Amen

Day 27: Maintaining Connections

"Family links us to the past while giving us a bridge to the future." –Unknown

"You're going to change so much." My mother spoke these words to me all those years ago before my young husband and I drove away in our packed car for our first military move. I fought it. Every part of me did not want those words to be true. But it's nearly impossible to move half a world away from your family, experience different cultures and a different way of life, and not change in *some* way. I had to learn that moving forward didn't mean I was betraying my past or those I loved.

If you move away from your hometown, as most military families do, it's often harder on the ones left behind. You'll be busily experiencing new things, leaving a hole where you were. Subsequent visits can also be challenging, with expectations high and intensity even higher if you're all staying in the same house. It's different than visiting Grandma and Grandpa in the same town and everyone going back to their own beds and space by evening. Staying in touch as much as possible between visits will help, as well as being emotionally prepared pre-visit and not placing unrealistic expectations on your extended family.

With our oldest now on active duty, I have the perspective of both sides of this coin. While I respect their privacy, I also long to be in touch with my son and his wife, a part of their world in whatever way I can. One thing I often say (and have said) to my kids is, "I'm just figuring this out, so

I know I'm not going to do it perfectly. Bear with me and forgive me!" Extending that grace to our own family is easier now that I see how tricky it is from this side.

Basic Training for Spouses

Staying in touch may be important to you if you have a close-knit extended family. Figure out what works best for your situation—weekly video calls? Texting often? Social media? (In another decade, there will be different options entirely!)

For older relatives who may not be as acquainted with social media, schedule time for a regular call if you can. Time has a way of getting away from us and you can end up going weeks or months without talking. I used to send a postcard to my Nana, my last living grandparent, from every trip we took. After she died, we found them in a bundle by the chair where she always sat. She obviously enjoyed looking through them over and over and it wasn't until then that I realized how much they meant to her.

Create a year-at-a-glance scrapbook. Utilizing online resources, print this out for several relatives or create a digital scrapbook and send links. You can also set up photo "albums" on social media and use the settings to make them only visible to the family members you choose (because we all have that crazy cousin who doesn't need access to every part of our lives…).

Remember birthdays and holidays. You don't have to go all out or make it expensive, but letting your family know you remember them on their special day or during the holidays can mean so much.

Balance visits home with your own family's time. This was probably one of my greatest challenges when we first married. Any time we had off, I longed to spend with my family. But with little money for plane fare and a driving distance of over 20 hours, this wasn't often practical. As the years went on, we also realized that we rarely went on "vacation," only home for visits (and hey, the roads and planes run both ways!). Finding the right balance between visiting extended family and personal vacations is not a military-family only issue, as evidenced by all the *National Lampoon* vacation movies! It's important to come up with a vacation plan that is comfortable for you and your spouse and not be swayed by "have-tos" or guilt trips (this term takes on a whole new meaning!).

Visits home may have an underlying pressure you wouldn't normally experience if you lived nearby and saw each other more regularly. Lowering your expectations and extending grace will go a long way toward alleviating some of this. Remember that their lives have had to go on, too, and things will not be exactly as they were when you last saw them. If you're staying with family, plan for some outings with just your spouse and children to give everyone a break and help with some of the intensity.

Scripture

"But Ruth said, 'Do not urge me to leave you or to return from following you. For where you go I will go, and where you lodge I will lodge. Your people shall be my people, and your God my God. Where you die I will die, and there will I be buried. May the Lord do so to me and more also if anything but death parts me from you' " (Ruth 1:16-17, ESV).

"But the lovingkindness of the Lord is from everlasting to everlasting on those who fear Him, and His righteousness to children's children, to those who keep His covenant and remember to do His commandments" (Psalm 103:17, NASB).

Think About It

Which of your family relationships could use some extra attention right now?

Is there something you can do to keep in better touch with extended family or friends?

Prayer

Dear Lord,

Help me to learn from my past and be grateful for where I've come from and the lessons I've learned. Let me appreciate what you're teaching me as we grow our own family in a different place.

Amen

God Is There in the Small Moments

Day 28: Searching for Beauty

"Think of all the beauty still left around you and be happy."
-Anne Frank

While stationed in Germany, a couple of my children and I took a trip to Amsterdam and had the opportunity to visit the Anne Frank house. The tour was somber and the visitors hushed as we climbed the steep, narrow stairs to the hiding place where the Frank family, Jewish citizens in danger of being sent to the concentration camps, had hidden during World War II.

If you don't know their story, they--along with others-- spent several years in a cramped apartment above their former family business and managed to hide from the Gestapo through the help of several trusted friends who provided them with supplies. As I walked the small rooms, I imagined attempting to keep children quiet while the workers went about their business below, and how stifling the boredom and isolation must have been at times.

In *Anne Frank: The Diary of a Young Girl,* Anne noted how the family did their best at keeping up their reading and studies and even did calisthenics to maintain strength. During our tour of the house, I was able to maintain my composure until I came upon some pencil markings on the wall, now preserved behind glass.

It suddenly struck me that what I was viewing decades later was oh-so-familiar to anyone who's raised children. There, Anne's father, Otto Frank, had taken time to line up his children every so often as parents do to measure their heights. Each careful marking included a date and the initials of that particular child. I could just hear a childish voice ask, "How much did I grow, Papa?" I was no longer able to contain the tears as I witnessed this attempt at a semblance of family life in the midst of the chaos and evil that had literally turned their lives upside down. And I think sometimes since that moment...*if the Franks could make that sort of an attempt, who am I to ever complain?*

This is not to say that we can never admit when we're in the midst of a challenging situation. Not at all. The lesson for me, however, is to always look for a way through a tough time, even when it's not readily apparent. A sort of "fake it till you make it," if you will. How can we do this?

Basic Training for Spouses

Find one thing that's normal and focus on that. If you're mid-move, maintain the same bedtimes for your children. If you've recently moved into a new house, cook a favorite family dinner, hang up a familiar piece of art right away, or plant the same type of flower that you had at the last place. Whatever it is, create some sort of touchstone for your family.

Do the next thing. At times, life can be overwhelming with the enormity of whatever you're facing: a move, parenting alone for months, missing family and friends. *Do the next thing*. Don't survey the entire problem, situation, or scenario at once. *Just do the next thing*. Fold one load of laundry. Drop the kids off at school. Run one errand. Go to work without thinking about anything except the next hour. *Do the next thing*. The rest will follow.

Live today. Don't allow the worry over what's to come ruin your time with your loved ones today. It feels like limbo when orders still haven't dropped, anticipating a homecoming, wondering just exactly how many birthdays/anniversaries/holidays your spouse is going to miss, but fretting won't change any of these situations. It's normal to think ahead and wonder, but don't let worry paralyze you from living completely *today*.

Scripture

"Therefore I tell you, do not worry about your life, what you will eat or drink; or about your body, what you will wear. Is not life more than food, and the body more than clothes? Look at the birds of the air; they do not sow or reap or store away in barns, and yet your heavenly Father feeds them. Are you not much more valuable than they? Can any one of you by worrying add a single hour to your life?

And why do you worry about clothes? See how the flowers of the field grow. They do not labor or spin. Yet I tell you that not even Solomon in all his splendor was dressed like one of these. If that is how God clothes the grass of the field, which is here today and tomorrow is thrown into the fire, will he not much more clothe you—you of little faith? So do not worry, saying, 'What shall we eat?' or 'What shall we drink?' or 'What shall we wear?' For the pagans run after all these things, and your heavenly Father knows that you need them. But seek first his kingdom and his righteousness, and all these things will be given to you as well.

Therefore, do not worry about tomorrow, for tomorrow will worry about itself. Each day has enough trouble of its own" (Matthew 6:25-34).

Think About It

When considering the Frank family or other similar stories of overcoming adversity through faith, what is the greatest lesson you take away from it?

What is one familiar routine that helps your family feel secure during times of change?

Prayer

Dear Lord,

Let me learn from the examples of others. I ask that you allow me to see my situation through different eyes. Thank you for the little touches of normal that bring a fresh view of life, even in the midst of challenging days.

Amen

Day 29: Roses in the Desert

"Hope is faith holding out its hand in the dark." -George Iles

I grew up in the Southwestern U.S. with its contrast of barren desert and stunning mountains. Brilliant blue skies were the backdrop of my growing up years. My mother was an avid gardener--honeysuckle trailed down a trellis in our yard, and I can vividly recall the lush flower beds and rose bushes. As a child, it didn't occur to me that roses pushing through the cracked, dry soil might somehow be incongruous. I never thought then about what difficult work it must be to sustain such beauty in the midst of austere surroundings. We moved houses several times in my childhood, but the yard and flowers were priorities soon after getting settled into the new place. That is a slice of my childhood: freshly cut lawns, immaculately groomed bushes, and beautifully maintained flower beds. I can close my eyes even now and breathe in the smells.

I've stopped counting how many houses we've lived in since we've been married, because it depresses me if I give it too much thought. When we move into a new house, I'm determined to get unpacked quickly and have things "in their place." I'm eager to hang curtains and arrange pictures, because I know it doesn't feel like home to my family without these familiar items. (Remember the example of Ma Ingalls in *Little House on the Prairie* setting out her china shepherdess as soon as the family arrived in a new home?)

Another aspect of creating our home is making an attempt at gardening. Even though it's a running joke in my family that not many plants survive my green thumb attempts, we still make an effort. I plant the bushes and flowers, even though I know that it won't be our family enjoying them in a few years.

But we do it. Because in performing these domestic, life-affirming chores, we feed hope and bring normalcy to our lives as a military family. If we didn't move forward with life at a new location, I believe it would affect our children and cause them to lose hope.

Hope is what makes you put out a pot of petunias in the spring when you're not sure you'll see the autumn in the same location. It's what makes you sew curtains for one more odd-shaped window. It's what makes you plug into one more church, one more social group, and one more neighborhood. *Hope* is what makes you extend the fragile hand of friendship again, when you've just said goodbye to the best friend you've ever had.

Hope is what makes you plant roses in the desert.

Basic Training for Spouses

Hope is defined by Webster as a "feeling of expectation or desire for a certain thing to happen." When I talk to other military spouses, there seems to be several common themes of things we're hoping for: our loved ones to stay safe, to find our place in the community we're currently in, for our kids to be ok.

But hey, you might be saying, *I can't just sit around* **hoping** *all day. Sometimes you have to act!* And I agree! But consider this. Whatever you're hoping for, God has planned so much more!

One of my favorite verses reads:

"Now to him who is able to do **immeasurably more** than all we ask or imagine, according to his power that is at work within us, to him be glory in the church and in Christ Jesus throughout all generations, forever and ever! Amen" (Ephesians 3:20-21, emphasis mine).

Wow! Now I am no theologian by any stretch, but just picture it. Whatever you're wishing for, God has so much more planned. Whatever good thing you're envisioning, God is currently working in your life in ways you couldn't imagine. We should be jumping up and down with excitement when we consider this!

I don't know about you, but that image brings me to tears when I think of a loving Father who not only knows my heart's desires, but One who so tenderly cares for me in ways I couldn't dream up myself. We can't even begin to scratch the surface of His goodness.

I often think of answers to prayer as *good, better, best*. I might think I need something that is *good* for me, while God has something *better* planned. The perfect answer to any prayer is God's *best*, of course, which is when I realize his answer is *better* than my *good*... which is *best*. Ha! That may not make sense to anyone but me, but hey...

God loves you! And that is a hope worth holding onto.

Scripture

"Take delight in the Lord, and he will give you the desires of your heart" (Psalm 37:4).

"But, as it is written,

"What no eye has seen, nor ear heard,

   nor the heart of man imagined,

what God has prepared for those who love him" (I
Corinthians 2:9, ESV).

"We rejoice in hope of the glory of God. Not only that, but
we rejoice in our sufferings, knowing that suffering
produces endurance, and endurance produces character,
and character produces hope, and hope does not put us to
shame, because God's love has been poured into our hearts
through the Holy Spirit who has been given to us"
(Romans 5: 2b-5, ESV).

Think About It

What is currently your greatest hope?

How can we differentiate between a good thing we're
hoping for and things that might not be the best for us?

What area do you need to pray that God will help you
relinquish what you think is *good* for what is *best*?

Prayer

Dear Lord,

Thank you that you always give hope, even in the middle of a desert. Help me trust in you, that you have my good in mind, even when life doesn't make sense. Help me cling to your promises and trust in your Father's heart to me.

Amen

Day 30: A Tapestry of Grace

My life is but a weaving
Between my God and me.
I cannot choose the colors
He weaveth steadily.

Oft' times He weaveth sorrow;
And I in foolish pride
Forget He sees the upper
And I the underside.

Not 'til the loom is silent
And the shuttles cease to fly
Will God unroll the canvas
And reveal the reason why.

The dark threads are as needful
In the weaver's skillful hand
As the threads of gold and silver
In the pattern He has planned.
                        -Corrie Ten Boom

I mentioned in the reading "Searching for Beauty" how my family and I visited the Anne Frank house in Amsterdam. But I wonder if you are familiar with the story of Corrie Ten Boom, which occurred during the same era? If not, I highly recommend you read *The Hiding Place*. Corrie was a single woman living with her sister and father in Holland during the opening days of World War II, while Hitler's armies drew ominously nearer to their peaceful village.

Though not Jews themselves, Corrie's father determined he couldn't stand by and do nothing while their friends and neighbors were murdered, so he chose to modify a closet in one of their bedrooms to hide Jews, dubbed "the hiding place."

While they saved many lives, the outcome was tragic for the family. Betrayed by an informant and sent to concentration camps, both Corrie's father and sister died. While there are similar stories during that time in history, what stands out to me about this one is Corrie's faith and forgiveness, even to those who had done her so much harm. She was known to often repeat the words from her sister Betsie, "There is no pit so deep that God is not deeper still."

I learned the words to the above poem "The Tapestry" when I was a young military spouse, after suffering my second miscarriage. They were painted on the wall of the church we attended at the time. Even though I didn't know who'd written the words, I often pondered their meaning for my life; the reminder that God sees the whole picture was a great reassurance to me. I didn't have to figure it all out. I could trust him.

Walking into the Corrie Ten Boom house in Holland, seeing the poem printed there, and realizing she was the one who'd written the poem that had often inspired me was so personally meaningful for me. Viewing the tiny hiding place in person and thinking about what the family and others had been through and considering the later forgiveness she'd extended to her captors, I experienced the Spirit of God and a feeling of hope which still fills that place--something I didn't expect to find in a place of such tragedy. Why? Because Corrie and her family trusted that, no matter what happens on earth, God has a plan.

Basic Training for Spouses

When I was younger, I remember accusing my dad that he too quickly forgave people who I felt had wronged him. I wanted him to stand up to them, to put them in their place. He gently reminded me that most people deserve a second chance.

Thankfully, I hope I have grown since that age! But, though I've walked with the Lord since I was nine years old, it is still not natural to forgive. It is not natural to bend my will to God's or even circumstances out of my control--whether it's an illness, or loss, or the inevitability of what the military dictates. If you find yourself in that place too, may I remind us both of some truths?

God is good.

God loves you.

God loves you personally.

God has a wonderful plan for your life. He loved you so much that he sent his own son to die for you so that you would not have to bear the consequences of sin. (See appendix for more resources.) What kind of love is this? *Crazy love*, as Francis Chan says--the same kind of crazy love that would cause a father to put his own life and those of his daughters in jeopardy to save others from a madman during World War II.

Can you trust that God knows, he cares, and he is carefully weaving the threads of your life together in a beautiful way? That is my prayer for you.

Scripture

"For his unfailing love toward those who fear him is as great as the height of the heavens above the earth" (Psalm 103:11, NLT).

"But God showed his great love for us by sending Christ to die for us while we were still sinners." (Romans 5:8, NLT).

"Greater love has no one than this: to lay down one's life for one's friends" (John 15:13).

"In the same way, we can see and understand only a little about God now, as if we were peering at his reflection in a poor mirror; but someday we are going to see him in his completeness, face-to-face. Now all that I know is hazy and blurred, but then I will see everything clearly, just as clearly as God sees into my heart right now." (1 Corinthians 13:12, TLB).

Think About It

During hard times, it can be tempting to see only the "dark threads" woven into my life, instead of the more difficult to see strands of silver and gold. In the days following my second miscarriage years ago, I couldn't understand what God was doing. It seemed senseless and cruel. I had to realize that I could not see the whole picture of my life; only God could. Have you struggled with this? How do you focus on God's goodness and not the circumstances?

For which part of your life do you have the hardest time understanding God's plan?

If you haven't fully given your life to the Lord and begun to walk with him, why not start today?

Prayer

Dear Lord,

Thank you that you have a good plan for my life and that I can trust your heart towards me. Help me to trust your goodness and your nature, even when the dark threads are all I can see.

Amen

Suggested Resources

There's so much available for military spouses! Realize that if you are facing a particular challenge due to military life, you're probably not the first. Don't miss these resources designed specifically for YOU! A bonus--these are typically free! For sites/locations funded by the military, remember that if we don't use those benefits, we'll lose them.

Chaplains: Each military installation usually has a chapel, with chaplains of various denominations. While the particular chapel style at your location may not be your cup of tea, chaplains are truly the pastors of the military family population and are there to help regardless of whether you attend services or not. Many installations also have PWOC (Protestant Women of the Chapel) and CWOC (Catholic Women of the Chapel) study groups.

MFLC (Military and Family Life Counselors): Short-term, non-medical, FREE counseling and referrals. Specializing in military life issues and completely confidential.

Family Support Centers: In the Air Force, we have Airman and Family Support Centers on our bases. Each branch of service has their own version of this (for instance Fleet and Family Readiness on Navy bases). They provide FREE help with resume' building and career counseling, along with numerous other services. Their staff is trained to talk you through educational and job opportunities, and answer questions you probably didn't even know you had!

MilitaryOneSource: Military life questions, education and employment, deployment and reintegration issues, military benefits, parenting, and confidential help 24/7. This is DOD funded. Log in to militaryonesource.com for hundreds of articles and help, as well as live chat if you need it or call 1-800-342-9647.

SECO: This is the Spouse Education and Career Opportunities section of the Military OneSource website. There is more here than I can mention: help with certification, scholarship opportunities, reentering the workforce, "virtual" work, and so much more.

Recommended Military Life Publications

Chameleon Kids: Support for the unique challenges military kids face, including the first ever magazine just for military kids, Military Kids' Life.

Military Spouse Magazine: The premier publication for military spouses. Read articles online, participate in their social media, or subscribe to the monthly magazine either digitally or print. (Full disclosure--I've been a regular writer for MSM for several years!)

SpouseBuzz: The spouse support section of Military.com. Online articles and resources.

Books Referenced

Anne Frank: The Diary of a Young Girl, Anne Frank (Bantam).

Crazy Love: Overwhelmed by a Relentless God, Francis Chan (David C. Cook).

Engaging Today's Prodigal, Carol Barnier (Moody Publishers).

The Hiding Place, Corrie Ten Boom (Chosen Books).

The Land Between: Finding God in Difficult Transitions, Jeff Manion (Zondervan).

The Little House Collection, Laura Ingalls Wilder (HarperCollins).

Endnotes

[1] Carol Barnier, *Engaging Today's Prodigal* (Moody Publishers, 2012)

[2] *The Land Between: Finding God in Difficult Transitions*, Jeff Manion (Zondervan).

[3] *Soul Surfer: A True Story of Faith, Family, and Fighting to Get Back on the Board* by Bethany Hamilton, Sheryl Berk, and Rick Bundschuh. Published by MTV Books/Pocket Books, 2006.